Penelope Frederica Fitzgerald

A Protest Against Agnosticism

The Rationale or Philosophy of Belief

Penelope Frederica Fitzgerald

A Protest Against Agnosticism
The Rationale or Philosophy of Belief

ISBN/EAN: 9783337070915

Printed in Europe, USA, Canada, Australia, Japan

Cover: Foto ©Thomas Meinert / pixelio.de

More available books at **www.hansebooks.com**

A PROTEST AGAINST AGNOSTICISM

"A PHILOSOPHY of belief, I do not mean of religious belief exclusively, or even principally, but of all belief, has yet to be constructed. I do not know that its foundations are yet laid."—*The Religion of Humanity*, an address delivered at the Church Congress by Right Hon. Arthur Balfour.

"The conscious realisation in the mind of an individual man of a philosophy or philosophical system must of course depend upon the actual intellectual development of *that individual*. The ultimate interpretation of self-conscious life and the universe which prevails among thinking men in any age or country thus depends upon the degree in which the *spiritual faculties originally latent in each of us are then and there drawn* forth into conscious exercise. When the higher spiritual faculties are left in their latency, as at birth, then the prevalent philosophy tends to a *self-contradictory scientific Agnosticism* and to *theological nescience*" (Professor A. Campbell Fraser). Faith is the correlative of feeling, intelligence, and will, and reflective reasoning therefrom. "Moreover, an honest attempt to comprehend the universe in the light of its *really ultimate conceptions* is the most arduous enterprise in which a person can engage. Its even partial success requires a *completeness in the verifying mental experience* which cannot be attained and sustained without the *fatigue which is inseparable from reflection;* and again our human individuality necessarily withdraws each of us from the *centre to a side view of the universal reality.*"

"What are all the sciences but the organised fruits of man's physical and metaphysical experiences?" *Presupposed to be essentially or ultimately reasonable*, together with the conclusions or inferences, inductive and deductive, that he *reflectively draws therefrom*. "Enfeeblement of reason sometimes walks hand in hand with worship of *mere* intellect." Locke, as the spokesman of the eighteenth century, was *unconsciously led towards a narrow and incomplete conception* of man and of *his insight of things*. "Emotion, thought, moral self-determination, and spiritual reasoning therefrom, these are the spiritual factors of philosophy, for on all these does the comprehensive settlement of philosophical questions depend. It is these that are the key to a metaphysical interpretation of the universe from the human point of view. 'These are the fountain light of all our day, the master-light of all our seeing.' Any philosophy which represents man only as ending in *sense* and *empirical* (or phenomenal) understanding, and as *generalising* only according to *sense* (impressions), must contain the seeds of *nescience* through its oversight of the larger human life that is due to the *factors of our spiritual experience.*"

"Life, Love, Light—these are symbols by which the mind apprehends the inexpressible central law, wings on which it broods over the unfathomed deep. Men will differ only in the several names which they will give it, according to *that ruling element in their several natures which gives them their contact with Divine things*. To have been fascinated *by one* of these vague symbols, to have made it *the summary of all thought*, and to have insisted on it even to monotony, has before now been recognised as the mark—*not of barrenness or ineffectuality*—but of an intellect deeply spiritual."

A

PROTEST AGAINST AGNOSTICISM:

THE RATIONALE OR PHILOSOPHY

OF BELIEF

.

BY

P. F. FITZGERALD

AUTHOR OF "ESSAY ON THE PHILOSOPHY OF SELF-CONSCIOUSNESS" AND
"A TREATISE ON THE PRINCIPLE OF SUFFICIENT REASON."

"I had rather not see another new face for a year, unless it were the face that shall
make all things new."—EMERSON'S *Letters from England*.
"I should utterly have fainted, but that I believe verily to see the goodness of the
LORD in the land of the living."—Ps. xxvii. 13.

LONDON
KEGAN PAUL, TRENCH, TRÜBNER, & CO.
LIMITED.
1890.

PREFACE.

My one object in addressing the public in each one of my works has been to show that our reflective self-consciousness of the faculties, or attributes of Being, is not only as legitimately the subject-matter of science as are the physical forces, but that, as the condition of all science, it claims the title of the science of sciences. For even in our trusting, or believing in the evidence of our senses, the exercise of the fundamental rational concepts of the understanding is involved, they in fact constituting our understanding.

Therefore we need not hesitate to follow the sense-transcending lead of our emotional, intellectual, and moral faculties, pointing as they do to the haven or heaven of our desire.

"Psychical laws are more radical than physical laws." It is psychical laws, and not mere physical laws of movement, that must furnish the ground of a philosophical theory of evolution.

75 CHESTER SQUARE,
LONDON, S.W.

CONTENTS.

A

PROTEST AGAINST AGNOSTICISM.

In my former works on Metaphysics, entitled respectively "An Essay on the Philosophy of Self-Consciousness" and "A Treatise on the Principle of Sufficient Reason," I have endeavoured to show the rationality of Faith, Love, and Hope.

The last work on which I have been engaged, has for its object the exhibition of the genesis of the fundamental concepts of the human understanding; but illness having impeded its publication, I am now offering to the public the introduction to it, as affording a *résumé*, or concise statement of my theory of thought, or spontaneous mental representation, together with my notion of reflective abstract cognition, and sense-transcending speculative inference therefrom.

Stated in a tabular form, my theory of the principles of mental representation stands thus:—

The idea or notion is of Being, which is apperceived in reflection on the three faculties, whose mental representations constitute the Principles of Thought, *i.e.*, the faculties of—

Feeling   Intelligence   and Will

(which is logically   (which is the con-   (which is the con-
the consciousness   sciousness or sense   sciousness of pur
or sense of   of relativity of   pose or sense of
Being).   Being).   tendency of
Being).

These assuming in reflection the forms of

Sufficient Cause.   Efficient Cause.   Final Cause.

Through which we have

Perception.   Apprehension.   Comprehension.

The synthesis of these fundamental modes in reflective conception is

Apperception,

which is of the whole Ego, Self, or *Subject-Object*; out
of which arises the logical or rational

Principle of Sufficient Reason,

which requires the satisfaction of our whole Being for
perfect Faith, Love, and Hope to be possible, and
affords answers to the all-embracing questions,

What?   How?   Why?

i.e., To what class does a thing or object belong?
How is it related to my Being?
Why, or to what end, am I so affected?

These must necessarily be consistent one with
another, and non-contradictory of the principles of
causality arrived at in reflective self-consciousness.

The *content* of consciousness is thus seen to be the sense of Being, or feeling, the sense of relativity of Being, or of the identity of cause and effect, and the sense of the tendency of Being, or of spontaneous self-determination in action ; whilst the *function* of consciousness is the recognition or perception of similars, the apprehension of causative relations, and the comprehension of purpose in others through intuition of the good for Being. *Thus only through the development of self-consciousness* is the evolution of the human spirit accomplished, the law of its evolution being the fulfilment or realisation of the reflective Ideals of Truth to Being, harmony with Being, and Goodness, or action beneficent to Being.

The objection to Metaphysics, that has hitherto been deemed unanswerable is, that the primary fundamental beliefs or axioms of reason have themselves no foundation *in facts*, physical, physiological, or psychological, being mere philosophical assumptions, or forms of thought, or mental representation, to which no realities correspond. Now, what I have endeavoured to show is, that the *actual substance* or hypostasis of thought is Being—the Being of the individual Ego presenting in every case the datum, or standpoint, of rational judgment and inference, or of mental representation. Natural or necessary representation being of the *subjective facts of feeling, intelligence of causality, and will,* which are seen in reflection to be the *à priori* grounds of the inductions or general ideas of reason—ratiocination being always in the ratio of Being, or relative to Being, which is the measure of subject-object mental representation. "Homo mensura" was one of the earliest doctrines of the Greeks. Thus on the temple of the Delphian Apollo it was written, "Know thyself," that being the condition of all positive or direct knowledge. What other test of reality have we, I confidently ask, than the witness of our own feelings and intelligence of causality? and what cue to purpose in action but our own? Affection involves the idea of substance, and the effect is of the nature of the cause.

It is out of the simple essential elements of self-love, social and divine, that our idea of duty, or what ought to be done as in obedience to the Makers' design in our creation, and in the creation of the universe, is evolved. "Gefühl ist alles," said Goethe. Self-neglect is suicidal. Want of sympathy with kind is idiotic, and indifference to, or conscious defiance of, the Divine order or will is wickedness.

A theory of Idealism[1] must, of course, treat of the genesis of the ideas of reason, which in their abstract form, or as abstracted in reflection from Being, or its experiences, constitute the abiding ideals of the truth, beauty, or harmony, and moral purpose in

---

[1] "Reflective thought is subjective reaction upon the multiplicity of experience that passively accrues." The idea of causality arises from the interaction of spirit with the material organism when the apperceptive or synthetic activity of consciousness is at work. Thus are the mentally constructed world and the real world or world of actual experience correlated.

action, in which the Supreme Ideal of perfection of Being consists, and which is the standard under which the life of a cultured, or fairly-evolved human being is normally conducted. The faith, love, and hope of a rational Being have indeed no other ultimate ground but these characteristic attributes of Being. Thence only do we predicate justice and benevolence of the Supreme or Prototypal Being, or the rationally and so necessarily postulated Sufficient Cause of the universe. Inconsistency with reality—*i.e.,* unreality—is logically *not* or *non*-Being, and self-delusion is obviously the admitted sign of irrationality or folly ; as action contrary to good feeling, and real knowledge, is always regarded as contemptible, because immoral ; for as approbation is the sentiment attendant upon goodness, so immorality arouses in us the sense of disapprobation, or righteous indignation.

Mental representations are now known to have a vital basis in the vital presentations of the nervous system, with its peripheral, or afferent nerves of perception, its sensorial centre, and motor centre connected with the muscular system, these conditioning our sensibility, and the grasping of similars in images according to personality, together with the activity of the efferent nerves, or nerves of conation, or self-determination for the carrying out of the will—upon these wait memory and imaginative representations, together with our judgments, and reasoning therefrom. The world of logic is the world of rational inference from the facts of our experience.

Thus the three elements of real Being, *i.e.*, 1st, The sense of personal power; 2nd, Intellection of relativity, with concomitant attraction or love for similars; and 3rd, Benevolent volition,[1] constitute the *rationale* of the categories of Sufficient, Efficient, and Final Cause, under which we recognise Being, understand casuality, and determine ourselves in action, the material frameworks of time and space effectively completing our mental representations. Dr. Munsterberg says, "The physical series of nervous events bears the whole of the causal strain."

The three fundamental and two subsidiary internal senses, Memory and Imagination, answer to the five external senses of our physical organism :—

(1.) Perception, which is accompanied by
      { (2.) Memory of former impressions, and
      { (3.) Imaginative objectification.
(4.) Apprehension.
(5.) Comprehension.

As each external sense has its respective physical function, so each of the spiritual senses has its allotted psychical office.

By the word *apperception* is understood the result

---

[1] Mr. G. Romanes, in his " Mental Evolution in Man," speaks of the transition in the mind of the child from "receptual, or non-conceptual ideation, to conceptual ideation," of which Self-consciousness is the required condition, being equally observable in the evolution of the race.

of the combined activity of the working and reflective forces, the representation, **as a** whole, of the five faculties of the soul. As real Being is, however, itself indivisible (the abstraction of its attributes being **only** a device for facilitating thought, **as** numerals are), it is only by reflection **on the sub-**ject-object that we can **arrive at a** Sufficient Reason for any faith **that is in us.** The only absolute **truth for** us is the Self-evident.

Real Perception, as opposed to phenomenal, or sense perception, is the act by which we recognise Being, or Existence in some way similar to our own, Sufficient Cause. for only through its relation to us, is it know-able by us. It proceeds upon the Principle of Sufficient Cause for a spiritual, or real effect produced **in us.** A table, chair, or stone causes us **no** spiritual emotion, but only sensation, **which is but molecular motion.** Hallucinations result merely from either disorderly *physiological* or psychological conditions **of our** nervous system ; but for true perception, a **sufficient, or** noumenal **cause,** is required, conditions not being *vera causæ*.

Noumenal, or intelligent Being may be made **manifest** to us through both physical and spiritual signs, for **we recognise** emotions in others by certain indications in their countenances of emotions **we have** ourselves experienced, **or of** sensations which different physical elements excite in our sensorium. Our capability of being intoxicated, **or** poisoned through the introduc-tion **into the brain of** foreign material substances makes sad havoc with its orderly, or normal activity, which can be thus either paralysed or over-stimulated. Still, as our experience, or the experience of the race, has shown us, these are but passing states of disorderly consciousness, ceasing with the morbid state of the nervous tissue, produced by abnormal physical growths, or decays, or by spiritual impressions of too overwhelming a kind. The normal function of the brain is orderly mental representation, which acts evolutionally upon it, whereas stoppage means disorder, as does also the disassociation of the three elements of thought.

It seems a truism that the absence of reason, or irrationality, is insanity; but if it indeed be so, how seldom *are any of us perfectly sane?* "If

Sanity Rationality. each of us had our deserts," says Shakespeare, "who of us would escape a whipping?" But even if the whipping be administered, *which it invariably is*, in some form or another, what a quantity of unconscious unreason do we still go on exhibiting! Were the Supreme Directing Power ever irrational, how could *we* understand anything? seeing that all appeal to our understanding is through our faculty of reasoning, which is always from our *emotions*, our static *intellect*, and our *will*, just as we reason concerning the nature of a material object from the evidence of one or all of our external senses. Only the rational is intelligently experienced by us, or can leave a lasting impression with us. "Philosophy," said Descartes, "takes the form of a reflec-

tively reasoned criticism of internal experience."
The being that possesses reason naturally, or by
the necessity of its nature, recognises reason in a
design, comprehends its final cause, or moral purpose, and in such recognition sees involved the
existence of an Intelligent Designer or Noumenon—
both wisdom and goodness being the attributes of
personality.

We only gradually advance more or less, each one
of us, into the light of *Self-Conscious Personality*, and
only then do we realise true self-possession,
or possess our soul in peace. Professor Self-Conscious Per-
sonality.
Campbell Fraser says : " This *self-conscious*
life, between birth and death, *is virtually our uni-*
verse for each of us, knowable by each (only) under
certain (peculiar) conditions." Reason is the efficient
cause and explanation of the prevalence of law and
order in nature, just as it is the explanation of all our
constructive activities, social co-ordinations, and political constitutions. Thus also the world of sense and
natural agents presupposes the constant agency of a
rational Creator : natural, as well as supernatural, or
spiritual, evolution testifying to the immanence in
the creation of Supreme Reason, and the purpose of a
perfect or benevolent will. Matter appears to be the
condition of the manifestation of reason, revealing
as it does an underlying spiritual Substance, or Personality, one attribute of personality answering to
another as " deep unto deep." Thus only to man, out of
all the animal creation, are the power, the wisdom, and

the goodness of God manifest through the *self-reflective* reason, with which He has Himself endowed us.

Apprehension is the act by which we recognise relations, primarily between the Subject or Self and external objects, and secondarily the relation of one thing to another, or of a thing to a person, or of one person to another person. It proceeds upon the Principle of *Efficient Cause;* for an immediate effect can only be produced by the mutual action and reaction of essentially associated, though it may be unconsciously, associated, factors.

Efficient Cause.

Efficient Causation holds an intermediate place between the Principle of Sufficient, and that of Final Cause ; the relative minor or objective relation being the link between the two, which stand towards each other in the same relation as do the major premiss and the conclusion of a syllogism.

No good thing can be attained, unless the right means for its attainment are employed, and it is obvious that unless there is an intimately conceived, already designed, *end to be attained*, no adjustment of means would be possible.

Comprehension is that act by which we recognise the essential tendency of Being. It proceeds upon the Principle of Final Cause, or normal intention, or intuitive purpose in action. Since everything we do is invariably with the purpose of satisfaction, or the supposed satisfaction,

Final Cause.

of Being, we cannot *rationally infer* a purpose other than this in the activity of other Beings or in the Divine activity. And as perfect satisfaction argues a perfect Being, the ultimate aim of reflective reason must of necessity be the endeavour after subjective perfection of Being, by means of the culture of the reason or understanding, and the search for general information, as also through sedulously acting always up to the degree of moral enlightenment which we have already attained; for, as Jesus taught, only those who do the will of the Father, as far as they already know it, are capable of receiving a noble doctrine. In vain does the sower scatter seed upon the hard high-road, or upon too superficial a soil; and even when the soil is favourable, the rain must fall upon it and the sun must shine on it; and, in the case of human character, the ploughshares of adversity must upheave it.

But it is only in reflective self-consciousness, that the mind abstractly conceives causation, sufficient, efficient, and final; for apperception concerns man's emotional, intellectual, and moral nature, hence only can he state to *what* class an object belongs, *how* it stands in relation to himself, and *why*, or with what purpose, it acts or happens. When we speak of the will of God as happening to us, it is not that we regard it as haphazard, but because we are powerless to contravene it. Still He has placed a witness to His goodness within us in the Principles of Thought.

By a Sufficient Reason for any judgment, or for

any inference drawn therefrom, is understood the synchronous corroboration of the three normally represented principles of causality :—

(1.) Being, or perceived Sufficient Essential immediate causality.

(2.) Relativity of Being, or apprehended efficient mediate causality.

(3.) Tendency of Being, or comprehended final causality, *i.e.*, rational purpose comprehended in all noumenal activity.

The Principle of Sufficient Reason is therefore the test of the validity of our opinions, and of the worthiness of our actions and character. Seeing the vast amount of enjoyment there is in life, Pessimism seems a doctrine without a sufficient reason; but did the life of man end here, Optimism would be equally so, because of the amount of suffering experienced in it.

The simple understanding seeks only *Cause*. It is the reflective principle of apperception, or self-consciousness in man that makes him ask for a *Sufficient Reason* for the existence of any thing, Being, or event; the Sufficient Reason always being the satisfaction, fulfilment, or actualisation of self-conscious Being.

The *rationale* of this, that, and the other, being by the terms its relativity to, conformity, or *correspondence with the nature of Being as such, or per se.* A sufficient reason is one that satisfies the whole of our nature : the heart (feeling), intelligence (understanding of causality), and the typical will (which is the desire for the best for Being, or the perfection of Being). A right course is one that leads to a good end.

"This is the Ideal, or Eidolon of worthship (value or trustworthiness) which is of sufficient causality to sustain the superstructures of science and philosophy." It is by the fundamental axioms of reason that individual opinions

The Ideal or Eidolon of Worthship.

or suppositions are tested. The mode in which things appear to each of us is, however, strictly *relative* to our individual faculties, conditioned as they are by our particular neurotic diagram. Logical representation is *necessary* representation, as being typically rational representation, the correlate of the neural *presenta-*tions of causality. It is the intuitive internal sense of Ideal Perfection that produces yearnings—yearnings for love, human and divine, yearnings for certain knowledge, absolute faith, and the concomitant hope of love and faith. The pivotal ideas of evolution are first made manifest in the instinctive straining after progress.

It is in choosing between his own various instincts and impulses that man exhibits what we call *free-will.* The question is on each occasion, What is his really proper line of self-determination ? Shall immediately pleasurable sensation or emotion prevail over our intelligence of Sufficient and Final Causes,

over truth to the nature and destiny of noumenal
or spiritual Being? No gain of comfort in our
sensations or of immediate enjoyment of emotion
can result in the really *best* for Being if the moral
laws of benevolence and duty towards our Creator be
left out of account. It is from the co-ordination of
the three principles of causality that we arrive in
reflection at the sense-transcending inferences concerning the whence and whither of man, as also at
answering the wherefore of our sufferings here. If
perfection of Being is the goal, "surely the way is
good leading to this!" Want and suffering are the
stimulants to mental or rational activity. *Qui veut
la fin, veut les moyens.*

It is quite as logical to inquire, What will be?
or what was rational? as to inquire into
what it is rational *now* to do. Hence we
say, This is what must happen, or have
happened. Our statement of the freedom of the
will may thus be made: "I can now *choose to
do what I conceive as right or reasonable, however
strong may be my inclination to act unreasonably.*"
But it is only when I stop to *reflect* on the consequences of any course of action, that I am likely
to represent to myself the irrationality of it. Consequently Reflection is *the true seat of conscience,
or the sense of duty as opposed to mere persistence
of inclination, &c.* "Freedom is the *ratio essendi*
of the moral law, and the moral law is the *ratio
cognoscendi* of freedom." A strictly rational inter-

*The must be
is of Reflec-
tion.*

pretation *is a disinterested interpretation, because it relates to pure* **Being** *as such,* not to *you* or *me* in particular. Kant said of the moral law that it is the sure and only sufficient *evidence of freedom,* and that the test of goodness as a motive, is whether that motive could be adopted as a universal principle of action. Man's evolution lies in *the evolution within his mind of the fundamental truths of reason, i.e.,* of the three principles of causality, and in that of the *reflective principle of Sufficient Reason,* which is the Principle of Personality.

Absolute determinism is incompatible with the sense of duty or responsibility, or the logical existence of the word *ought.* Our reflections may be but shallow, still they give rise to some sort of ideal of Being; and it is to this, our *own ideal* to which *we ought* to be true, it being our duty to our Maker to be true to the actual sense of Being, with which He has endowed us. It may be that we have but one poor talent, but we are none the less obliged by conscience or the sense of responsibility to our Maker to be true to this, *i.e.,* to exercise it. It is true that *our choice lies between rational judgment and irrational inclination;* but it must be remembered that individual judgment is the result of an inherited neurotic diagram, modified by the social medium to which the mental organism has been subsequently exposed in the course of its evolution. Hence my theory of the perennial requirement

[marginal note:] Determinism, according to Ideal Choice.

of an eternal spiritual counterpart or opposite. Hence, *le besoin d'aimer*, the yearning of the lonely soul for its *complement*.

Were it not for our intuition of causality, belief in the existence of an external object would not be possible. This intuition arises in us out of our own power to produce effects, hence we infer that there must exist power as Sufficient Cause for the production of an effect upon us. Mere physical *force* is not the synonym for *power* which invokes intelligence of result, and purpose. In all knowledge of substance, whether spiritual or material, there is involved knowledge of designing, adapting power. Wisdom is the sense of relativity, and goodness is action according to power and wisdom. Self-evident conceptions are necessary conceptions, and what is cognised in self is *recognised* wherever it appears or is exhibited. Rational satisfaction is of the needs of feeling, of intellection, and of the moral sense or sense of justice and benevolence. These are our standards of judgment and of conduct, but, weak and ignorant as we are, one of the chief requirements of reason is the frequent suspension of judgment when evidence is insufficient.

Only in reflection do we consciously realise and idealise our experiences, ideals being abstracted from Substitution of Similars (*see* Jevons). our own experiences together with those of the race. A Supreme Being is revealed to the mind solely by *reflective conceptual* recognition, or necessary logical "substitution of similars." We recognise immediately in sense and perception a physical organism like our own, from its similarity to our own material organism, and we recognise the passions of anger or joy through their signs in the distortion of the features, or in the placid sweetness of their expression, we ourselves having experienced like nervous modifications of our attitude and countenance. Thus in reflective contemplation of the attributes of power, wisdom, and goodness manifested in our own Being, we rationally assume the existence of, or substitute, a similar Being — only Supreme, Prototypal, and Absolute, instead of relative and finite, such as we are, to account for our relative existence and for our notion, or rational idea of the universe, physical and spiritual. To Him alone, we attribute the perfect equilibrium of the attributes of Being, in which perfection of Being consists. In our own dual or sexual creation, "which is the supreme form of the principle of polarity which pervades both the spiritual and material universe," we behold the Divine provision for our approaching somewhat nearer to the required equilibrium: opposite polarities being necessary complements of each other's existence. "True love is the outcome of complementary characteristics."

All relation is primarily conceived by us as with our own Being, and secondarily as between other persons, or different things. The sexes are correlative. The first exercise of the intellect is differentiative : through feeling we have the intuition of relation between real cause and effect, as opposed to conditional existences. Only a baby can feel angry with a heavy book for falling upon it, or with a table that is pushed against it ; for by the terms of the two propositions, these articles are incapable of malice towards it, being only the conditions of its being hurt, not the real designing causes of its suffering.

A condition is not a cause.

In the case of an earthquake or of the fall of a house, the law of gravity is referred by the adult to the Constructor of the Cosmos to account for the earthquake, and in the other case some finite Being is asked to explain the negligence or folly that has occasioned our being hurt ; for *well-being* is intuitively assumed to be the object of the order of the universe, and of the conduct of men ; only the moral maniac delights in the sufferings *of others*, only the *fool in his own*, unless they are undergone voluntarily for the gaining of a higher good, or nobler and truer happiness.

The substitution of similars, or necessary or logical representation of a similar cause for a similar effect, is the natural intuition of the human understanding with regard to the existence of *other spirits or rational Beings*, whilst material external objects are revealed to man through his own physical organism, which conditions his spiritual evolution, and thus fits him for ultimate blessedness.

Through reflection on our own Being, in its various

aspects and modifications, we are able to *re*-cognise similar modifications of Being in the relations of human history and biography. The correlate of the idea of right is that of duty.

There is certainly nothing to be wondered at in the prevalence of Agnosticism amongst those who neglect the culture of reflective introspec- Being, the tion, for the idea or conception of Being as Pivotal Fact of the Uni-
an abstract notion, only arises out of reflec- verse.
tion on the three faculties represented in the principles of thought, *i.e.*, *feeling*, *intelligence*, and *will*. These are what we call the attributes of Being : its properties, or qualities, as we say of material substances. The idea of attribute involves that of a spiritual subject, as physical properties suppose a material object of thought, or mental representation.

Thus Hegel speaks of the identity of thought and Being : thought consisting of the representations of the modifications of our own Being in feeling, intelligence, and will, as also in sensation, Thought psychologically speaking. Thus, when we
say, "I think this a clever performance," it is as if we said, "I *feel its effects* (for only through *the operation of things upon our faculties do we know anything*), and am consequently induced by it to certain particular modes of feeling, thought, or action." The nature of any fact is not known in its full reality unless we know it in all its relations to the system of the universe, or, to repeat Spinoza's expression, "*Sub specie æternitatis*," as regarded in

the light of eternity. The proof of belief in a doctrine is acting up to it, or in accordance with it. Carlyle speaks of " living in the burning light of Infinity and Eternity." It is the type or ideal standard of Being which the *generalisations of* reason reflect, and hold up to us as the *abstract* standard or " Counsel of Perfection," to which we, and all others have to conform. It is the attributes of Being that furnish the categories of thought. "The categories of thought are the primary moulds into which thought is cast " (Laing).

Reason holds the scales, giving each part of our Being its due ; egoity, or self-reverence, being properly balanced by sympathy or altruity, the combination of both of these, together with adoration of the Divine will, in thought and action constitutes our duty to God, He having so ordained the constitution of our reason, that the moral sense or categorical imperative of action witnesses to His own goodness or benevolence towards all Beings.

As the major premiss of a syllogism contains its conclusion, so the Idea of Being involves *that* of the end, or aim of the activity of Being—viz., the conservation of the integrity of Being. Evolution, which is through the relativity of subject to object, and the converse, represents the *means to the end of perfection of Being.* The interaction of

Rational Consciousness.

subject and object is in this wise : The action of the object upon the subject evolves passion, or emotion in *the subject,* and

the reaction of the subject upon the object evolves
moral volition, when reflective **reason is brought** to
bear upon the problems of life. Reflective reason in
its *recognition* **of** *similarity and* " *substitution* **of**
similars" is the mother of the **sciences ;** in its representation of equivalence, correspondence, symmetry,
and *proportion of parts to a whole,* it is the *fosterer*
of the arts, and in its *logical insistence* on action
being *in accordance with these intuitions, so as to*
fulfil the Divine order in the universe, it is the
source of the moral sense, or sense of Justice.

" Rational activity, or activity in conformity with
the law of the world, is directed to the attainment of
the greatest possible happiness for one's self Life and its
and the whole world" (" Life," by Count Evolution.
Lyof Tolstoi, p. 139). The subject of all reasoning
is the subject-object of *apperception*, or reflective **self-**
consciousness. "The object of all courses of reasoning determines *the order* in which the separate trains
of thought must be arranged." Man studies *life only*
in order that it may become better." " Those men
who have advanced humanity have not abandoned
the aim of reasoning." " What I really *know* is the
suffering which I fear and hate, and the pleasures and
joys which I desire—*the consciousness of suffering*
and of enjoyment, and of aspirations towards good-
ness is the chief sign of human life." " I cannot
imagine life otherwise than as a striving from evil
towards good." "The chief *definition of life, which*
is its aspiration towards happiness, is *discovered*

only in the consciousness of man" (Tolstoi). "At the awakening of his intelligent consciousness (reflective reason) man regards his past conception of life as a mere animal existence, or one in which his whole idea of duty lay in the exercise of his profession or business. Man's real life begins only with the appearance of rational consciousness." " The whole of man's complicated, seething activity, his trafficking, his science, and his arts, is for the most part only the thronging of the unintelligent *crowd about the doors of life,* who go away after being jostled there, under the full conviction that they have been of the assembly" (Tolstoi).

If, as Jesus said, "we cannot cast out Beelzebub by Beelzebub," so also, from our conception of the moral law, we cannot but impute goodness or holiness to our Creator. If all professed Agnostics were suddenly deprived of reason, they would then, and only then, be justified in *asserting that they know nothing.* Are not persons who understand nothing called idiots or madmen? " I reflect, therefore I *know that I exist—I know that I know*" (Descartes' Axiom).

The general term *things* includes the physical conditions of Being, or sensitive presentations in our mental representations, as time, space, and extended bodies. Our own material frame is properly used in connection with the word *existence* as opposing the outer world to the inner, ontological, essential, or real world of life. Only pure Being *is* enduring, because it is of the **essence of** the Prototypal Being, " begotten, not **made."**

Matter is the Proteus, ever shifting in form, and so apparently dissolving. Existences are merely phenomenal, passing away like images in a dream. Sensible consciousness and sub-consciousness are liable to be interfered with by disease of physiological tissue, they not forming a part of the essential, enduring substance of the spiritual representations which reflective reason apperceptively *re-represents.* " Being *alone* endures ; intervals of time, of one minute or 50,000 years, are indistinguishable by *it*, because for it, *time does not exist.*" Noumenal, or real Being alone gives intelligibility to the external Cosmos or material order, of which the only *rationally conceivable raison d'être* is for the evolution and manifestation of the power, wisdom, and goodness of Spiritual Being; the struggle with matter in its various forms being the school for the development of rationality in finite spiritual beings, through which the power, wisdom, and goodness of the Supreme Prototypal Being, by the logical substitution of similars, becomes more and more revealed to, and participated in, by us.

Seeing that each one's own Being is the only thing *positively,* instead of *indirectly,* or inferentially, known to any one of us, how can we arrive by logical induction at faith in the existence and essential nature of the Supreme Being if we decline to reflect on our own Being ? For what is all objective knowledge but *re-*

cognition of similarity and difference to our cognised self, or Ego? No one is surprised at a person's ignorance of the science of chemistry, if he has not studied the subject, or at a man's ignorance of, or incapacity for, the art of music, when he has an uncultivated ear and hand. Why, then, are people to expect the science of **metaphysics,** or ontology, obviously the deepest of the sciences, to be anything but mysterious to a person who neglects the *culture of reflection,* and of the *reflective self-knowledge,* which has been endeavoured after by the ancients, alike of the East, and of the West, as the touchstone of the validity of all other information that can possibly be reached— only our own human nature affording a sufficient reason for our faith, our love, or our hope of a happier future? How but through using the faculty of sight do we even see the glorious sun? the image to man of the *splendeur de Dieu,* by which Henri IV. asseverated his assertions. And can a man be expected to recognise the activity of an intelligent powerful Moral Being in the creation, if he has neither reflected on his own Being, or on Being in the abstract, as the one source of power, wisdom, and goodness?

As we know in this world that further knowledge of any subject does not entail, or mean the contradiction of what we already know, so it is with regard to our actual knowledge of the attributes of our own spiritual, noumenal, or real Being, together with our comparative knowledge of other beings, and our superlative knowledge of the Supreme Being. It is not rational, *i.e.*, according to our experience in Being, to suppose that we shall ignore elsewhere what we have known, loved, or hoped for here. Above all, how can the two that *are the complements of each other's Being forget* each other? This would be no resurrection of our true selves, but like a fairy-tale metamorphose of a woman into a cat. The passage from one extreme of climate to another may disorganise our physical system, and so dislocate our mental representations for a time; but we do not find, as a rule, that the passage from one country, or district of government, to another permanently disturbs our spiritual relations with those we love and honour, or develops in us a desire for lovelessness, ignorance, and wickedness, immorality or unhappiness. Why, then, should our passage to another star essentially affect our spiritual nature, although the external circumstances there may subsequently prove more *rapidly* furthering to our spiritual evolution?

"God," says Locke, "when He makes the prophet, does not unmake the man." The *Being* of man, or the existence of man apart from relation to a Supreme Absolute Being, is unthinkable. Relationship implies obligation to sympathy or kindness, particularly in the measure of the kindness or goodness shown to us by another. Who, then, has been so good to us as the "Author of all good things"?

When sense, or sensuality, takes the lead of soul, or spirituality, we have a degraded Being, one out of whom the *virtue* or spiritual essence has departed. Marriages contracted through the lust of the eye and the pride of life are of the earth, earthy, and consequently cannot be supposed to be held binding in a world, "where dwelleth righteousness," they being in no way in harmony with real Being or morality, however respected by, and dear to, conventionality they may be here. Small wonder is it that priests, or spiritually-minded men of various religions, have sought refuge from such ties in the cloister. As to women, they have chiefly been driven to the convent by their relations, so that the estates of the family might remain unencumbered by them; therefore we cannot give them much credit for spirituality in the matter, most of their actions, whilst in a state of bondage, being more like those of serfs, than like such as behoved the better half of man. It is now being maintained by scientists that Naturalism, or Secularism, is a sufficient basis for morality. What I am endeavouring to show is, that this is untenable and that in man's rational or spiritual nature *alone*, is found a sufficient basis for morality, the duty of purity being involved in man's apprehension of relativity to a Supreme Creative Being, who has *absolutely*, or in perfection, the attributes of Being, which, although possessed by us only in a finite,

Sufficient Reason for Faith, Love, and Hope.
limited, imperfect, and physically conditioned degree, yet constitute us the spiritual offspring of the Father of Spirits. The only Sufficient Reason for faith in the Supreme Being

is the rational evidence of things unseen by the eye of sense, but which are " the substance of things hoped for."

The reflective ideal of mind hinges upon spontaneous feeling, intelligence, and will, which are psychological facts, just as seeing, hearing, and smelling are physiological facts. As we must have a reason for the faith that is in us, so we must have a reason for our love, and for our hope, unless we wish to forego being rational creatures. Thus reflective inference takes its stand upon the actual nature of Being. Pure reason has only to do with the attributes or qualities, which are the indications of pure Being, of which matter is only the condition of manifestation. What reflective Reason claims as her own, is inference, or conclusions, from judgments arrived at *through the association* of the elements, or principles, of thought, which I have enumerated under the heads of perception, apprehension, and comprehension. Apperception is the reflective perception of the whole of Being in the indivisibility of the subject-object which is the object involved in all perception, apprehension, and comprehension, all argument being from it, inasmuch as it is the one datum for all inference of reason, just as the five physical senses are called into play exhaustively to perceive a sensible object. It is the internal *I*, or Ego, that perceives, apprehends, and comprehends respectively the Sufficient Cause, the

Ideal Mind; Pure Reason.

Reflective Reason is Synthetic Thought.

Efficient Cause, and the Final Cause of whatever is in question, arriving through the triform Causal Principle at the apperception of the Sufficient Reason of our Faith, Love, and Hope, in ourselves, in our rational compeers, and, above all, in our Creator, Preserver, and continual Benefactor. Feelings, ideas, and desires that are contradictory of the rational ideal of Being are like the house spoken of in the New Testament, which, being built upon the sand, the winds beat on it, and the waves washed it away, leaving no trace of it behind, because of its having no real place, or place of enduring fulfilment in the universe. Such feelings, ideas, and desires are but arbitrary tricks of fancy, sometimes seemingly charming, but not really beautiful, because not in harmony with spiritual or real Being, whilst oftener they are monstrous and hideous travesties of it. The only really Efficient Cause of true Love, or spiritual attraction, and for a certain hope of joy in another and happier state of Being, is the *actual experience* of the *perfect joy of sympathy, in this life*, in which lies the perfect fulfilment of our own self-conscious Being, from its being made *whole* or *holy* through union with its correlative spirit ; and in the reflective deduction therefrom of the nature of our destiny from the nature of the Creator, the pure and Holy Being in whom we live, and move, and have our being ; and Faith, in *Whom* is the substance of things hoped for. In Him there is no shadow of change, no possibility of self-contradiction, so that we may "rest in the Lord," sure that "He will give us our heart's desire," He Himself having so constituted us that we must fain desire completeness, which is holiness of Being—one-sidedness, or partiality of judgment, constituting injustice, or imperfection of Being.

Judgment, and reasoning therefrom, cannot be conducted apart from the *association* of the Ideas of Causality in combined introspective self-reflection. "Eines Mannes Meinung ist keine Meinung, wir müssen hören beide" (Inscription over the entrance of Rathhaus at Frankfort). The sense perceptions must be supplemented by an actually active intellectual element, before they can yield any true perception; therefore sensation alone, is not true consciousness, but only the sub-consciousness, or the unreflective imaginative consciousness of the lower animal. A sensation involves chronological and spatial relations, commonly called time and place. The conditions of sensation are physical or material. We intellectually assign the sensation, actually experienced, to the action upon our nervous organism of some material object. For a physical effect, a physical cause is postulated. Psychological consciousness, as opposed to ontological or spiritual consciousness, represents psysiological or phenomenal causation, as well as noumenal or real causation—our sensational as well as our emotional experiences, the latter, alas! being often so fatally conditioned by the former. The word "necessity" is simply a logical term applying only to ontological

Judgment and Reasoning.

Sensation.

or spiritual concepts, as opposed to passing or accidental sensations ; but in the early history of the
race, as in Fetishism, Polytheism, and Judaism, we
find the idea of a Supreme Being confused with
Anthropology, or the conception of the animal form
of man.   Sensation is the material on which the
intellect works.   Imagined sensations or hallucinations are the product of some neurosis initiated within
the higher or lower nerve centres of him who experiences it.   Out of them has arisen the common
belief in apparitions or ghosts.

The word "logic" essentially denotes the theory of
argumentation.   Pure logic treats of the *rationale* of
thinking, *i.e.*, of the avoidance of self-con-
Logio.   tradiction.   Applied, or verbal logic has
chiefly for its office the avoidance of mutually contradictory forms of speech.   Self, or Being, is thus
the standard of truth or reality of conception.   John
Venn, the logician, says : " The extraordinary variety
of general conception and exposition of which logic
has proved to be capable is now pretty well known.
The illogical may scoff at this as a sign of chaotic
uncertainty, but logicians rejoice at it as a proof of
vitality and healthy growth."   Inference is from the
known to the unknown, by means of some point of
relation or similarity between them.   By *inference*
is meant conclusion from evidence.   To quote again
from John Venn : " Mr. Spencer recognises the science
of reasoning as *subjective*."   Mr. Spencer uses the term
" science of reasoning " as a department of *psychology*

in his " Principles of Psychology." Except under the influence of reflecting minds, the knowledge of the true order of the three laws of causality would hardly have been attained ; witness the hideous superstitions of the ignorant. The ideal of science is truth, or Sufficient Cause. The ideal of æsthetic, or emotion, is corresponding harmony, as Efficient Cause or means to the end, or Final Cause of goodness of existence, *i.e.*, the best or most blessed for Being. Being is the pivotal fact of science ; Love, or the harmonious attraction of Beings for each other, is the typical emotion of Being, and goodness is the moral result of the religious sentiment, which is to us the key to the understanding of the Divine order of the universe. Thus equipped within, with the Ideals of Truth, Beauty or Harmony, and Goodness, should man descend into the arena of practical social life. It is the *reflective ideal of Spiritual Evolution*, which offers to us the *rationale* or rational solution or Sufficient Reason of our trials and struggles and sufferings in this poor little planet. This is the reading of " the riddle of the Sphinx," which, unless a man read, he must be torn to pieces.

Logic is thus really the science of *knowing the before, and after, through the actual, or present.* As Hegel said : " Thinking or knowing is one with Being ; " and the great utterance, " The logical postulates are the predicates of God," is due to the same author ; for what is thought but the representation of the various modifications, aspects, or attributes of our Being? A thing, or object of thought, *realised out of our own consciousness of Being, is the inconceivable by reason,* as being a self-contradictory representation. The lower animals are in every way as far from being exhaustively comprehensible by us from their being below, or less than our own consciousness, as is the Supreme or Absolute Being, from being so infinitely above our own finite, conditioned consciousness; and as *only* what is known through its relation or correspondence with ourselves or similarity to us in the lower animals is comprehensible by us, so only through that part of our nature which is related to the Divine, or Perfect Being, are we able to conceive and realise His existence. Only an intelligent and powerful Being can recognise power and intelligence exhibited in what he beholds around him, as only a benevolent Being can recognise benevolence in any creation, or arrangement. To the gnat, or the beetle, the order of the universe is not patent: for them no cosmos exists—mental conception being, like physical conception, "after its kind." Perfect mutual understanding is the result of mutual equivalence of nature, hence the correlation of spiritual counter-parts (Wahlverwandschaften).

Each man is what his ideals represent; he cannot jump off his own shadow. In the writings (translated by Giles) of Chuang Tzu, the Chinese moralist after Confucius, and the reactionist against his Positivism or Secularism, there is the following interesting dissertation on Reason, or "Tao," as it is rendered in the Chinese language.

In the Chinese cosmogony Yu and Yang are the positive and negative principles from whose inter-action the visible universe results. Confucius said, "All that a fish wants is water; all that a man wants is Tao (Reason). In *Tao* life and death are one. A man said to Nu Yu (by one authority reported to be a woman), 'You are old, and yet your countenance is like that of a child. How is this?' Nu Lu replied, 'I have learnt Tao.'" (Emerson is said never to have lost his youthfulness of character.)

"Could I get Tao by studying it?" asked another. "I fear not," replied Nu Lu; "you are not the sort of man! There was Pu Liang, who had all the good qualities of a man of science, but not Tao."

"Meng Lun," said Confucius, "has made an advance towards Tao, wisdom, towards Tao, wherein there is no weeping nor gnashing of teeth. Tao may be attained, but cannot be received." As Emerson says, "To know a thing, you must get to it." In the New Testament we have, "This sort cometh not but by prayer and fasting." "Tao has its own evidences, its own laws." "Before heaven and earth were, Tao was. It has existed without change from all time." The long chain of proximate causes makes for *finality* in Reason; they are *the means* to the beatitude of Being. Reason is that which informs all creation. It is of all phenomena the ultimate cause, *i.e.*, there is a Sufficient Reason for all existing phenomena in the nature, and requirements of self-conscious Beings.

The *word* is the embodiment of the notion, or idea. "It is the creation of the mind and the best evidence of existence." But for the rational process of mental representation how should *we know* that we exist? "*Je pense, donc j'existe*" (Descartes). "*The unknowable thing becomes a thought under an idea of Reason which the word expresses*, enabling us to communicate it to others, and to retain it ourselves as a symbol of a reality. "Language is in a manner the embodiment of Reason." "Many a word will be found to rest on some deep analogy of *things natural and things spiritual*, bringing these to illustrate each other, and to give an abiding form and body to both. "He who first discovered the relation was a poet" (Trench)—a relation meaning harmony, as that of musical notes, or as the analogy between a physical and spiritual storm, or upheaval.—Language is the mirror of the inner living consciousness. The object is revealed to the subject through a mental synthesis of memories and images under the fundamental ideas of Reason.

"The mind must bring with it the categories which make Nature intelligible." *The mind*, or rather *Being, brings with it the idea of reality*, by which it judges appearances. It also brings with it the sense of Relativity and of Finality.

(Marginal note: The Word is the Expression of Reason.*)*

"Science seems to question Nature *by an idea* which it takes to Nature" (the idea of Being or of the modifications of Being). The question is, What are the principles on which experience must be questioned, in order to attain real knowledge? Only the knowledge of Being, and of what relates to Being, is real or intelligible to us. A madman's story, all sound and fury, signifying nothing, is deemed unreal. We cannot rationally believe contradictions of Reason, by the terms.

Being is the Pivotal Science: all Argument is from Being.

St. John says, "In the beginning was the Word, and the Word was with God, and the Word was God." "In Him was Light, and *the Life was the Light of men.*" That is, *Being* is the Light of all our seeing. "I am that I am." "My name is I AM;" and in Him, the Supreme Ideal Being, we understand in some degree the great plan of the universe as the abode of rational spirits in different stages of evolution, all being prepared for communion with, and rejoicing in Him.

Reason represents Being.

The following quotations are from the Chinese book already cited :—

"There is a state, that of Tao (Reason), in which killing does not take away life, nor does the prolongation of existence add to the duration of life. Fu Yuh obtained it, and, as the Minister of Wu Sing, got the empire under his control, and now, charioted upon one constellation, and drawn by another, he has

been enrolled among the stars of Heaven as representing *Genius.*"

"It is easy to be respectfully filial, but difficult to
be affectionately filial—the artificial is easier than the
natural."

"The Yellow Emperor said, 'Perfect music first
shapes itself according to a human standard, then it
follows the lines of the Divine. I played as a man
drawing inspiration from God; the execution was
punctilious, the expression sublime.'"—*Chuang Tzu.*

Of the existence of *feeling* we have the most intimate and immediate knowledge, for *we ourselves are
feeling*, as we say, "God is love," or *Divine feeling.*

Emotion the Psychologi-cal Aspect of Feeling. (I feel cold, means I am cold.) "Feeling is
a fact; it is the most indubitable fact of all,
and all knowledge rests on it. Psychology
takes this fact as the basic datum of its investigations,
and must attempt to reduce all more complicated
phenomena of psychic life to simple feeling" (Dr.
Paul Carus).

Impressionableness is another name for feeling.
The physiological, as well as the psychological, condition of memory is that impressions be left on our
physiological or psychological substance. The nerves
of animals being centralised in the brain, their feelings form a multifarious unity which is called consciousness. The *reflective* consciousness of man, or
apperceptive self-consciousness, is what distinguishes
man from the lower creatures. When we speak of

spirit, we speak of enduring Being, or, as Emerson calls it, *real* Being, without any reference to the bodily forms in which it manifests itself, varying from the minute frame of the infant to the full-grown man—varying no doubt still more in different stars.

It is the spirit of man *that looks* for the fulfilment of its faith, love, and hope *hereafter;* the present exhibiting, partly through the weakness of the flesh, *almost the reverse of the ideal of the perfect* and *the blessed life,* even when the spirit is willing or prepared for it, excepting for some brief hours in which

> " The soul's delight takes fire,
> Face to face with its own desire,"

in the presence of its spiritual or eternal affinity.

By the very term *soul,* it will be understood that I am speaking of the soul, or spirit's desire, not of the lusts of the flesh, of which it is spoken, "Earth to earth and dust to dust." When feeling, intelligence, and judgment are in perfect harmony through the correspondence of objective presentations with the triple ideal of these attributes of Being, and its conceptual representations of fulfilment of Being, or spiritual desire, then and there, in whatever place or state such fulfilment or perfect satisfaction of Being occurs, we are in Paradise or the place of happiness. Our idea of hell is a negative one, meaning the place where happiness is *not.* It is awful to realise with Schubert's "Der Wanderer," "Dort, wo du bist

nicht, dort ist das Glück." Shakespeare says : " It is
sad to have happiness dawn upon us *first* in the eyes
of others." It is obvious from this that, according to
the opinion of the present day, Shakespeare lagged
far behind George Eliot and Carlyle in nobility of
sentiment ; only we must remember that in Shakespeare's day the doctrine of loving one's neighbour so
much better than oneself had not yet been broached.
Perhaps if the old-world lesson of not sacrificing
others to ourselves, were thoroughly learnt first, it
would be better, as it would be acting upon the
principle of "being just before we are generous."
Walter Scott says of love, "And Heaven itself de-
scends in love, for love is Heaven, and Heaven is
love."

Count L. Tolstoi says, in his work entitled "Life,"
" Man possesses in the depth of his soul an efface-
able demand that his *life shall be happy*, and have
a rational meaning." " The time will come when a
rational consciousness will outgrow false doctrines,
and man will come to a halt in the midst of life, and
demand explanations." " I desire happiness, I desire
life, I desire rational sense, but in myself, and in all
who surround me, there is evil, death, and incohe-
rence. How am I to live ? What am I to do ?"
" As there is no contradiction in the seed, which
sends forth a shoot and then dies, so, on the awakening of the rational sense in man, there is no contradiction, but only the birth of a new Being, of a new
relationship of the rational sense to the animal"

(Idem). "All we know in the world, we know only because that which we know is consonant with the laws of that reason which is indubitably known to us." "There is no measuring without a measure."

"The most important knowledge to man is the knowledge or elucidation of the law of reason, to which, *for our happiness*, our animal personality must be subservient. It is evident that the knowledge of this law he can nowhere procure, except where it is revealed to him, *in his rational consciousness*." "We know fully only our own life, our aspiration for happiness, and *the reason which points us to that happiness*" (Count Lyof Tolstoi). "*Reason is represented by the law of organism in ourselves and the lower animals.* We recognise in them the same striving towards happiness" (Idem). The happiness, or *bien-être* of man differs from that of lower animals, in that *it means for him* the *fulfilment of the Ideals of Reason*—as *Faith*, or trust in the integrity of spiritual Beings; *Love*, or the sense of harmonious relations between the subject and spiritual objects; and *Hope* in their goodness and unchangeableness; above all, in the goodness and unchangeableness of the Supreme Being, the Father of Spirits.

"The true life of man, *from which* he forms for himself an *Idea of every* other life, is the aspiration towards *happiness* attainable by the subjection of his personality to the law of reason. It is only in the increasing *attainment of happiness* by submission to reason that what constitutes the real life of man consists." " Man will never understand a life of which he is unconscious. We know (certainly and only) the law of our rational consciousness, which we must fulfil." " In the real life of man, body and matter, the two forms or modes of existence bound up with his life, furnish him with implements and materials for his work, but not the work itself." It is in the spiritual union, and communion which we call love, arising out of the attraction of like for like, that *true joy* consists, whilst the perfect *rest* and *trust* in which happiness lies is to be found only in the adoring acceptance of the Divine Will.

Count Tolstoi continues : " Life is a striving towards good ; a *striving towards good is life.* Thus all men have understood, do understand, and always will understand life." " The common herd of unthinking men, believe the welfare of man to lie in the welfare of his animal part. *False science* excludes the conception of happiness from the definition of life, agreeing with the error of the masses in seeing the happiness of life only in animal welfare." " *Rational consciousness includes Individuality* in itself, but individuality does not always include in itself rational consciousness." "Man's rational consciousness shows him that the satisfaction of his animal individuality cannot constitute his happiness ; *therefore his life draws him irresistibly towards the happiness that is peculiar to him*, and does not

become confused with *his animal individuality.*"
" The sole actuality of happiness for him being only
of such a sort as may be satisfied by his rational"
(*i.e.,* reflective) "consciousness" ("Life," by Count
Lyof Tolstoi). " Rational consciousness requires that
our actuality should be directed to striving for the
happiness of others, as well as for our own." [1]

All reflective reasoning is based on a complete
assent of all the faculties, or through their representation of the presentations or modifica- The Neuro-
tions of the nervous system, owing to the tic Diagram.
impressions made on the individual brain of the
reasoner from without, and to the consequent reflex
activity of the same. Each person has his special
neurotic diagram, or cerebro-nervous conformation,
such as it has been transmitted to him from his
ancestors, and as it has been subsequently modified
or evolved through the peculiar social medium in
which his early and later youth has been passed.
An individual to whom the scientific, æsthetic, and
moral senses have been feebly transmitted is as insensible to æsthetic, intellectual, and ethical sentiments, and as little able to appreciate emotional,
intellectual, and moral truths, as a person born
colour-blind or devoid of an ear for music is able
to appreciate the exquisite beauty of æsthetically

---

[1] " In Aristotle's 'Politics' we learn that the object of all action is
happiness ; not understood in a hedonistic sense, but as the complete
development of man's higher nature, conditioned by the modera-
tion, and within certain limits, by the satisfaction of his lower
impulses."

combined colours or the harmony of melodious strains.

Such as these can scarcely be said to have awakened to the life of emotion, intellection, and moral purpose in this state of Being; whilst, again, there are other natures open to all noble enthusiasms for the true, the beautiful or harmonious, and the good, which to the undeveloped are sealed fountains. Some individuals in different families and countries seem "survivals" of a barbaric past, but eternity is long enough for the evolution of each and all of us; but as reflective reason is what distinguishes man from the brute, surely the sooner it is cultivated the better, the absence of it resulting in moral misery to the individual himself, and all with whom he is concerned.

Our inherited "neurotic diagram" (see Cyples) constitutes the fatal part of our destiny. Hence the personal equation has always to be made in the case of every judgment expressed concerning the blameworthiness of any individual, in the case of the wise, as well as in that of the foolish; for although the foolish constantly sport the opinions and wise sayings of others, their own foolishness must never be left out of account in our inferences from their so-called *expressions*, which are more truly *parottings* of the real expressions of feeling, intelligence, and will. Nor is even the wise man altogether, and always wise and good, being of mortal, as well as celestial parentage.

If it were not for the law of the association of the three fundamental ideas of reason, called by Professor Wundt the law of reason and consequent, there would be nothing but a perpetual kaleidoscopic change of feelings, an ever-transforming present, without past *The normal Neurotic Diagram presents the Forms Re-presented by Common Sense.* or future. In such case, there could be no abiding sense of relativity, and so of trustworthy judgment, no ground for our Faith and Love, and their concomitant Hope, of ultimate blessedness. The three associated ideas of causality, when combined in reflection, give clearness and stability to feeling, just as sounds regulated by the laws of harmony, remain in our memory, and as definitions of things are fixed upon the mind by articulated speech, or words. Comprehending the causes of an emotion, its suitability or compatibility with our whole nature, we realise it as an abiding possession. We can only properly *think* of what is a *possible*, or *proper* object of *thought*. Fancies and divagations are not thought, properly so called.

Special certainty is conditioned by individual reason. Logical or abstract certainty is ideal, just as in speech, logical and grammatical, a rational concept alone being truth to reason, is said to be *necessarily conceived;* the *What we call Necessary Truth is Conditioned by Human Reason.* fundamental concepts of the understanding being the only basis of demonstration.[1] With the

---

[1] These factors of the human understanding have a fact-ual basis of re-presentation in the normal presentations of the nervous system, as also in the re-representations of reflective introspection.

evolution of reason comes the solution of rational problems. Science deals with the general principles of reason. The truths of reason are *self-evident*. Boethius calls a maxim, "*Maxima propositio.*" All definition comes from experience. An arbitrary proposition or an *alogical sentence* or paralogism is not convertible into a self-evident proposition; why, then, should we accept it? Evidence being rational, axioms, like other general propositions, result from the reflective elaboration of particular experiences. Axioms relating to our corporeal or material experiences are called physical truths; spiritual or ontological axioms are called metaphysical.

In the treatise on Natural Philosophy by Professors Thomson and Tait, it is remarked that " physical axioms are axiomatic to those only who have sufficient knowledge of the action of physical causes to enable them to see at once their necessary truth." " A ploughboy," says Mr. Herbert Spencer, " cannot form a conception of the axiom, that action and reaction are equal and opposite—thus it is with *à priori* ethical truths." " An *à priori* system of absolute political ethics is a system, under which men of like natures, severally so constituted" (or evolved), " as spontaneously to refrain from trespassing, may work together without friction, and with the greatest advantage to each and all." As " the system of Ideal Mechanics is indispensable for the guidance of real mechanics," so it is with regard to social and political ethics. It is from abstract Ideals that we reason in reflection.

"In *attention*, the real Being, the noumenal, not the phenomenal Ego, gains the ascendancy Unity of the Ego. over the complex of its presentational (or neural) life, asserting the principle of its *oneness*, which is its own nature." Each separate cerebral hemisphere contributes an element of content to our simple consciousness of *affectional, intellectual,* and *active* purpose.[1] The unity is of the underlying spiritual consciousness; but when the cerebral centre is diseased, this is, alas! suspended. "*A man's opinion is what his entire systematic representations have made it;*" hence St. Paul says, Whatever is honest, whatever is pure, whatever is lovely, *think* on these things. Admitting that the mind is an organisation existing in intimate parallelism with the neural organisation by a pre-established harmony, we cannot from this single fact reduce either to the other. The products of the sense-transcending apperceptional synthesis have an objective realisation in the idea of Deity, the Ideal Being, the *Ente possibile* of Rosmini—that is, the Being *rationally or logically conceivable, and conceived as possibly existing*—this conception differing altogether in kind from *physical seeing*, which is conditioned in its exercise by the actual state of the sense-organs of the individual. But in our present state of Being both our physical and

---

[1] Schopenhauer and Professor Wundt resume the whole of mental representation in will.

cerebral powers are intermittent, as in sleep, they being deciduous, and secondary to the real Being of the spirit, by which man stands related to the Supreme Being, the Father of all finite *rational beings, whose knowledge of Him is the fruit of reflective reason,* His peculiar gift to them. Spiritual unity lies deeper than the functional unity of the nervous system, to which mind, or conscious mental representation, or thought is related, which therefore wavers in its action through its affiliation with an unstable physical system.

In the order of presentation, Being is first, as also in the order of Noumenal knowledge, the sense of Being meaning the *consciousness of emotional existence* and *power;* next comes *intelligence* of relativity, or of relation to other Beings; and then *will,* or autonomous tendency to *action* for the conservation of the integrity, or supposed perfection of Being. Emphatically *will* is the orientation, or determination of the rational mind to a statically conceived or *intuitively given end;* the natural organic, automatic self-determination for self-preservation *being the physical basis of morals.* Seeing that reflection is upon given facts of our nature, such as the sense of Being, the sense of the relativity of Being, and the sense of tendency of Being from which the ideas of causality are derived, it can bring with it no contradiction of natural science any more than it can of *ontology,* or metaphysics. Did reflection contradict common

Will.

sense, modifications of our *emotional* (as opposed to sensation), *intellectual*, and *moral* or spiritual being, could indeed have no place amongst the sciences ; for all speculative or metaphysical truths are as directly abstracted from the actual facts of our psychological experiences, as physiological and physical truths are from our sensible experiences ; and all inferences as to our whence, and whither, are drawn from them in introspective reflection on the nature of our own Being, and that of all other rational, or similar beings with whom we are directly or indirectly acquainted, through the reflective logical substitution of similars.

Out of reflection, in the comparison of these, arises the categorisation of the rational principles of mental representation or thought, which are seen in experience to be those of Being, relativity of Being, and final tendency of Rational Being, *answering to the neural presentations of Sufficient, Efficient,* and *Final Causality.* The last means always rational action, or action for the good or best for Being—the *Ding an sich und für sich*—the relations existing between the subject and spiritual or metaphysical objects, emphatically that of Love, constituting the Divinely-ordered means to that end. It is Love that makes life a path of light—" Love is the path, and love the goal ; " but one is often minded, with Shelley, to say that a new name should be found for the new birth of the spirit into spiritual harmony, so that it may no longer be confounded with the lust of the flesh or sensuality.

Perhaps nothing can be more curious than to hear persons or things decried because they have the properties peculiar to their kind or sort, seeing that, for a reproach to be logical, we should be able to assert of persons, or things that they are wanting in the essential quality which constitutes them members of their own class or kind, which gives them a name and place in the world.   Yet against Metaphysics it has been urged that, like the spider's web, it is *woven out of our own Being,* and therefore, strange to say, is charged with having no objective stability !   Certainly ontology, or Metaphysics is the science of the *Substance* or *Substans* of all direct or subjective cognition, and therefore obviously of all indirect or objective cognition or *recognition of similars,* in which spontaneous reason consists, just as in the reflective "substitution of similars" (see Jevons) lies the process of introspective reasoning *from self-consciousness.*

Truth is to Type or its Ideal, to which Governments as well as Individuals must Conform.

The three fundamental principles of thought or laws of the understanding—viz., the principles of Sufficient, Efficient, and Final Cause, in their synthesis in reflective reasoning, constitute the web and woof upon which all our experiences of imaginative, emotional, intellectual, and moral impressions are broidered.   They are, as it were, the skeleton, sustaining the ever-changing body of our imaginings and purposings, without which we should not be rational and speculative beings, seeing before and after. We can no more doubt our intelligence of causality than we can doubt the existence of our own feelings and volitions; the phenomena of feeling meaning effects produced upon us, just as our volitions are manifestations of the causal power of our own Being; but how can their subjectivity be an argument against their validity, seeing that subjective, or self-evidence is the only valid evidence we can produce upon any question. Through the *subject-object* or Ego, through its feeling, intelligence, and will alone, are all objects conceived or conceivable by us.

Logic has also been twitted with throwing no light upon the riddle of the Sphinx, viz., Whence comes man? Where goes he? What is the meaning of his troublous destiny here? Why is he the victim of "a most outrageous fate"? and when "a bare bodkin could put an end to his sufferings," why does he go on enduring them? Logic is contemptuously said to have no mission but to maintain the principle of identity, *i.e.*, what is, is: A is A; but it must not be forgotten that logic also involves the principle of contradiction: no A is not A; and the principle of excluded middle: nothing can be at once A and not A. These fundamental premisses, in the reflective synthesis, constitute the principle of *Sufficient Reason for belief*, making the solid ground of inductive and deductive conclusions. Most of the absurdities of private opinion, and even of so-

Logic is supposed to Consist of mere Truisms.

D

called logic, lie in the unconscious breach of these postulates.

Personality must exist in a perfect or infinite form in the Supreme Prototypal Creative Being, for Whom difficulties in the way of the execution of His benevolent will cannot exist; of Whom, temptations to evil-doing or evil-feeling, or ignorance of causality, cannot be predicated; Who, as all-powerful, all-wise, and all-good, must be impersonated Benevolence or Love; in Whom there can be no shadow of change.   Whereas it is we that, as imperfect, are *always " becoming,"* as Hegel said, or *being evolved*, as we now are through our struggle with material conditions, as also with our own idiosyncrasy, until it is equilibriated through union with our counterpartal half, so that we may not be weighed in the balance, and found wanting, as it is the dual, or social unit only that can reflect, however faintly, the full-orbed perfection of the Prototypal Being, the Father of Spirits, Who was, and is, and is to come; who, if the starry heavens were rolled up into a scroll and scorched to a cinder, as our own moon appears to be, would still exist, surrounded by the spirits of the just made perfect through great tribulation, not one tittle of His word or reason having passed away.   Only *the same Sufficient Reason could still be predicated for His creation of a new heaven and a new earth*, namely, the existence, delectation, and ultimate perfection, or *blessedness of self - conscious and God - conscious*

Infinite and Finite Personality.

beings; the order of the external, automatic *cosmos consisting in its* **strict relativity to intelligent,** *loving, and autonomous* **beings.** Who then shall say that logical inference, or the necessary conclusions of reflective reason from the three combined principles of causality which constitute our reflective reason, contains no prophecy of a *future* destiny for man, when his emotions, intellect, and moral sense will receive perfect satisfaction or fulfilment; for what is our dreamed-of heaven but the place of fulfilment of rational or Divinely-implanted desire? Thus the Jewish Scripture says, "Oh, rest in the Lord, and He will give thee thy heart's desire." Well might Spinoza say that everything should be considered *sub specie æternitatis,* in the light of the inferences of reflective reason, which are drawn from the nature of our spiritual or real Being, not from the caducous nature of our bodily animal organism; and until this emphatic doctrine of reflective reason (*i.e.,* the doctrine of the immortality of the soul) habitually controls the feelings, understanding, and activity of man, and is held to him as the ideal of duty, to bear it in mind from his childhood up, men will drink, and women will weep hysterically, involuntarily "sighing for what is not," for what they have not even a clear idea of, kicking against the pricks of a too outrageous fortune, which, unexplained, outrages their moral sense as well as their emotions and their understanding. Shall the creature be more *just,* *more wise, more benevolent* than his Creator? "Shall not the Judge of the whole earth do right?"

If a human being, for want of a child, adopted the child of another, and after having delicately bred and nurtured it, should cast it adrift and helpless upon the world, exposed to hardships with which he had rendered it unfit to cope, he would justly be pronounced a monster, *i.e.*, a man wanting in *humanity*, or reason, disappointing the child's faith and hope in goodness. Why, and how, then, should we fear that the Maker should despise his masterpiece, and desert the reflecting spirit, that through large discourse of reason sees before and after; and not vainly, but wisely or logically, sighs for what is not—*i.e.*, love, the love, wisdom, and goodness that are not manifested in perfection here? The old Zoroastrians pronounced those who lived in tents accursed, and Abraham is praised for seeking an abiding city with lasting foundations, a city wherein dwelleth righteousness or order. Should we not also deem ourselves accursed in a world, where all that is given is taken away from us, were it not from rational intuition of a heavenly or abiding country, a Paradise far more perfect than the earthly one? " I will restore to you the years that the locust hath eaten " (Joel ii. 25).

The Judgments of Pure Reason apply to all Beings, even to the Supreme as such.

John Stuart Mill, who maintained that if he were sent to hell for saying that eternal punishment was irrational as a punishment for *finite* shortcomings of duty, to hell he would **go rather** than deny a logical judgment, learnt **so to see the necessity of eternal** *Love*, through his **great** affliction **from the** loss of his **beloved wife, that he** maintained Love is the Fulfilling of the Law. in his **posthumous** work the rationality of Hope, *or expectation of the attainment of the desire of our hearts as an integral part of our mental constitution*, and consequently as a rational datum for inference of reflective reason, its office being to *re*-represent *synthetically* the spontaneous representations of the modifications of our Being, which is what we call thinking, and to draw transcendental or *sense-transcending inferences therefrom*. As David said, " Though Thou slay me, yet will I trust Thee." This mode of mental representation being peculiar to man, " Homo mensura ; " we have no other standard of conception but Reason. Epictetus said, " Have not the gods left the door open for you to leave this life when you please ? If the house smokes too much, we desert it." But Jesus taught us a better and a more truly logical way : The child who loves his father does not kill himself rather than endure his law, but trusts implicitly in the goodness or benevolence of that law ; therefore man in like manner should *endure unto the end*, naturally trusting that for such enduring, great will be the reward—this is the standpoint of all religions.

The Efficient Cause of evolution is the relativity of the object to the subject. Only through the constant action and interaction of the one upon the other, does evolution towards the Final Cause of our Being take place. Thus is the *wholeness* or perfection of our Being accomplished. Perfection is always after its kind ; the perfection of the logically postulated Absolute Being never being possibly attained by the relative or finite Being, and only *as opposite* extremes balance one another, man and woman *united* in perfect sympathy together faintly reflect the fulness of the Divine Being. " Give us of thy fulness, O Lord," says the Psalmist, " for with Thee is the fountain of life." " WHAT IS IT THAT I WANT, O MY GOD ? " says *a Norwegian song*, the refrain of which consists in the sad words, " *And the sun went down !* " It is wholeness of Being *through union with its counter-partal soul* for which each human spirit, even though it may be unconsciously, yearns. This is the lesson of reflective reason. The tradition that man was first created alone, and that it was not found for his good or his happiness to be alone, bears upon this point. Epictetus says, " When we give a cow good pasture, we do not expect *chewed grass returned to us*, but *milk*." The *pure milk of the Word*, or *reason*, is what God expects of us.

Werden : becoming. (Hegel.) Marriages that are made in Heaven.

A marriage may truly be said to be " made in heaven," when each of the contracting parties has really found his or her eternal complement in the other. Well has it been said, that " once to love truly is never to love again."

Marriage Eternal.

" Die Rosen, sie **blühen** jedwedes Jahr,
  Die Liebe blüht einmal, und dann **nimmermehr.**"

As no two **persons, or two minds, are exactly**
alike, so when two beings are exactly complementary to each other's spirituality, through the complicated **character of** the marvellous combination
of qualities requisite to bring about and sustain such
a conjunction, *there can be no* conceivable *substitute found* for it. "To say that *true* marriage is
in its nature divine, is only another way of saying
that *true conjugal love is of necessity eternal.*" The
Lord, *whose it is to give us ideals,* does not contradict His own ideas. Two hearts that feel as one,
responding to each other's thoughts, must be eternally
one in spirit. "What grows out of the body perishes
with the body. Love has little to do with it, for
Love is of the soul."—*Daily Telegraph*, 15th Decem-
ber (Robert Buchanan).

Mr. Montgomery says, "The perplexing question
of the *relation of thought to Being* is the essential
point on which, in its various phases, the
contention of modern thought is turning."
Now this is a question to which the present
work attempts to offer the key. The existences of
the earth, man, the universe, and even of God, are
gathered up into a logical whole in reflective reasoning. "La raison suffisante," meaning "La raison
suffisante à tout comprendre, parcequ'elle comprend
tout." *Being is Being. Matter is not noumenal*
Being. Nothing is at once Being and not Being.

Relation of
Thought to
Being.

Matter is only a condition of the evolution of *finite Being. Our possession of* the general principles of *rational demonstration* and of their synthesis in the principle of Sufficient Reason is *strictly relative* to our *own Being,* which is the one *strictly - known* POSITIVE : the *positive* being the necessary ground of the comparative, and the superlative concepts. This alone enables us to understand the world in which we live, and through analogy of judgment and inference, to embrace even the myriad stars in one comprehensive view of what we call the universe. It is the pre-established harmony, or relation, between the subject and object of representation, which prevents solitary monadism, or imprisonment in self; and arms us with the power of the spontaneous recognition of similars, and of the logical substitution of similars in reflective reasoning.

The mind or understanding is linked together with the nervous system by subjective causality, so as

The Subject of Consciousness.

to furnish the principle of Sufficient Reason for Faith, Love, and Hope. Where there is an impression made, there must exist something to receive the impression, and something intelligent to have made, or calculated an impression on us. To take no note of this is simply to ignore essential logical implications, such as those of inborn sense : as the sense of cold implies the sense of absence of heat, and the sense of darkness, the felt absence of light. It would certainly be a curious basis for any sort of doctrine or inference of reason, to ignore these truths of the understanding. "Whether a result of the intimate agglutination of sensorial particulars or a *product of the synthetical activity* of the *intellect, re-synthesised mental content* must *refer to something beyond sensible consciousness,* to its *sub-stans* or support." Thus it is obvious that the *subject that possesses and controls* the contents of consciousness must be of a *sense-transcending nature.* This is the subject which is endued with *permanency, efficiency, and a sense of final* tendency or will-power. Directly the soul leaves the body, the body begins to dissolve into its physical elements.

No valid science of psychical phenomena can dispense with a constant reference to realistic implications, *i.e.,* implications of a real or nou- Extra-Conmenal Being behind phenomenal conscious- sciousness. ness. Physical science, even in its most abstruse mathematical flights, confines itself to the investigation of time and space relations, or of sense-compelled naturalistic percepts ; but the realistic implication is of the Being who perceives, apprehends, and comprehends, the Originator of the efforts of the wonders of science, and the Imposer of the categorical imperative of Duty. "Representative psychical marks make up the conscious realisation of native individual sense." No marks can be understood without reference *to that, of which they are marks* or indications. Psychical manifestations imply therefore an *extra-*conscious or *real* Being, the *substans* of the varying phenomena of consciousness, and of the interruptions to consciousness, as in fainting or the distorted consciousness of madness.

"Pleasure and pain are '*quales*' or qualities of all presentations of the psychic life, as we know it.

Subjectivity of Pleasure and Pain ; hence the Hedonistic School of Philosophy.
Subjectivity is easier to grasp in the region of pleasure and pain than on any other ground." But subjectivity is in fact not so much of the matter, or that of which rises into consciousness, as it is of the reflective form of it. The action of nerves is the *objective condition of mentality*, which is subjectiveness. The cerebro-nervous system is the physiological basis of mentality ; when this is dislocated in any individual case, mental confusion ensues. Indifference is the state of neutrality between pleasure and pain. Here, by the terms, impressions are very faint, and so ineffective. "Pleasure is the mental side of efficiency and expansion. Pain is the mental representation of contraction, or lack of efficiency of Being." Sorrow is a form of self-pity, as well as of pity for others, just as joy may be either the result of gratified egoity, or of satisfied altruity, or of adoring gratitude to the Joy-Giver for perfect happiness. Alike egoity, altruity, and the religious aspiration after Deity and duty must be fulfilled, for the complete satisfaction of finite rational Being.

Besides physical pain and pleasure, there exist emotional, intellectual, and moral pain and pleasure. We have aching hearts, as well as aching heads, and distracted heads as well as saddened hearts.

Constrained attention upon intellectual problems partakes of the nature of physical fatigue. The moment sometimes comes when we say, " I *can* no more ; " and so deeply are our physique and morale interwoven, that when the heart breaks, the brain becomes a ruin. We have, as might be expected, a far deeper sense of enjoyment from the exercise of our spiritual *essential faculties* than from the gratification of our physiological or *organic needs.* It is in activity, not in passivity, that life rejoices. Even the representation of tragedies is said to be enjoyed, because we are made thereby to feel alive at the very core of our Being. The nature of Feeling does not admit of intellectual definition, intelligence only revealing to us its cause or causes ; only what is *felt* is really known, as also must be the sacred enthusiasm of duty, which is in its origin a part of the religious sentiment.

Feeling, Intelligence, and Will are the three irreducible facts or elements of the pivotal fact of Being, from them arise self-love, sympathy, and love divine. The being located in such a place or point of space is a small matter ; the question is, " Est-ce que l'on y aime toujours ? ou est-ce que l'on s'y hait toujours ? " In the one state of feeling we have Heaven, in the other Hell. The inferences of reflective or transcendental reason can never be wrong whilst they are logically drawn from noumenal data, *i.e.*, are true to the nature of our *spiritual* or

The Three Irreducible Facts of the Pivotal Fact of Being.

real Being; but in parotting a received doctrine, or traditional belief, we are apt to leave out of account some one or other of the elements, or attributes of Being, whereas right judgment depends on the fair and the full representation and satisfaction of them all.

Excitement, as the arousing of emotion, intellection, or volition, is so far pleasurable that it makes us realise our own essentially enduring and identical Being. The *ennuyé* seeks excitement for excitement's sake, the unemotional seeks sensation for sensation's sake. Emotional activity, intellectual activity, and causative or will activity are all pleasurable arousings of consciousness :—

"'Tis life of which our nerves are scant."

What wonder that man aspires, as does the flame, ever upwards, seeing that *mental evolution is the law of his Being!* Superstition is but the first, or rudimental, form of the religious sentiment, as conventionality is the first step to moral sentiment. I hold "the missing link" to be discovered in the merely sensual or animal man : the man not born again to the spirit, at least of conventional honour, if not to that of virtue and Divine aspiration after immortality.

Pain and pleasure are incompatible states. Hence a present state of pain or suffering is associated with painful memories, and a present state of bliss or joy is associated with the recollection of former states of joy. Thus works of imagination appeal to our painful or pleasurable experiences, aspirations, and anticipations. If we have not such, what meaning has poetry or art for us? If, like the French Margot, we only love the clink of money, even Nature has no charms for us. *Ni le cri de l'alouette, ni le chant du rossignol,* make any appeal to the worshippers of Mammon.

A state of consciousness gets all its definitions from previous representations in memory, which, of course, are coloured by our present state of consciousness. Byron says—

> "Joy's remembrance is no longer joy,
>   Whilst sorrow's memory is a sorrow still."

This is only true of a person who is unhappy in the present. For the sorrowful heart will echo past sorrows, but has no echo of a past joy; and in this world of vicissitude, this valley of the shadow of death, is not our sincerest pleasure fraught with some pain of memory or of fearful anticipation? Only through the peace which passeth this world's understanding or explanation—that is to say, only through the peace that springs from faith, love, and hope in God—can we know the rest of security even for the joy of spiritual love; for hope is its cradle and despair is its grave.

"It would seem as if the brain were like a very delicate photograph plate, which takes accurate impressions of all perceptions, whether we notice them or not, and stores them up, ready to be reproduced whenever stronger impressions are dormant, and memory, by some strange caprice, breathes on the plate." "Perception, however caused, whether by outward stimulation of real objects,

Sensorial Impressions.

or by former perceptions revived by memory, sends a stream of energy through the sense area, which, like a river divided into numerous channels, by expanding fertilises the intellectual area ; and conversely, the process is reversed when what we call will is excited, and the numerous small currents of the intellectual area are concentrated by an effort of attention, and sent along the proper nerve-channels to the motor centres, whose function it is to produce the desired movement." "This mechanical explanation leaves entirely untouched the real essence and origin of the intellectual faculties" (Samuel Laing, "A Modern Zoroastrian "). The ontological or metaphysical explanation of final cause or *raison d'être* of the existence of the mechanism itself is a strictly rational one, *i.e.*, one standing in essential relation to pure or spiritual Being, to which our corporeal frame and nervous system is rationally considered as strictly subservient. This is the triumph seen in martyrdom for love, divine and human.[1] Physical energy constitutes the fulcrum upon which our power to affect the physical world hinges. Reflectively regarded, it also appears to us as a *condition* of, or means to, our spiritual evolution, which is chiefly effected through suffering, together with the exercise of moral volition. As we carry within us the ideal of perfection of Being, or beatitude, as the Final Cause of

---

[1] Professor Huxley says in the *Nineteenth Century* (January 1890), when writing on the natural inequality of men, " Religions are the inevitable products of the human mind, which generates the priest and the prophet, as it generates the faithful."

Being, we are naturally roused to astonishment, curiosity, and even indignation, at the feeling of misery in ourselves, or at beholding it in others. We are thus compelled to make *every effort of intelligence and will* to avoid *suffering* and to attain to *perfection of Being*, which is Happiness. For we can but inquire, "Is there no Divine, or perfect order in the universe, answering to the postulates of Reason?" the categories of the understanding or the laws of thought equally enforcing upon us the idea of a *Sufficient* or Omnipotent *Cause for our Being*, our relations or similarity to whom constitutes the Efficient Cause of our being "lords of the creation," with the sense of an immortal destiny. "I think the thoughts of God," said the great French astronomer.

Reflection sets the seal of realisation on the knowledge derived from our experiences in spontaneous perception, apprehension, and comprehension. Consequently, the man who does not exercise his high prerogative of reflection does not, and cannot, be said, or expected

Our Knowledge only consists of what we consciously realise.

really to *know anything*, for he does not *know that he knows it*. In reflection we see how all objects derive their worth to us from the cosmical order of things, *and the spiritual ground of our sense-transcending* or Ideal conclusions. Truth is the correlative of feeling, intelligence, and will. But alas! not only our perceptual, but also our conceptual or reflective representations are liable to modifications through degradation of our tissues and muscular system, because they are involved in the actual status of the physical basis of our mental or spiritual representation. This is the true tragedy of man's life here below. " The spirit indeed is willing, but the flesh is weak." It is not from our physical mechanism, but from our real, or spiritual Being that the inferences of reason are deduced. This is what Giordano Bruno means when he says, " For I reason with none other than a natural soul," for reflective reason draws its inferences from this (see L. Williams's translation of " Gli Eroici Furori," by Giordano Bruno).

Apperception or internal perception is the special act by which knowledge of states of consciousness becomes possible. In reflection we know that we know. Like those of external perceptive, the inferences, internal, reflective, conceptive, or apperceptive, are *immediate, direct.* Only immediate physical pain is incompatible with the natural sweet peace and rest of faith and love, although patience and hope may lead us triumphantly through it to the peace of God, which passes carnal understanding.

Con-science is the first-fruit of being " born again to the spirit" of reflective reason. It is the revelation of reason that truth to Being, to relativity to Being, to tendency or finality of Being, is what *is required of us* by our Creator, is our duty to Him. Shakespeare says, " He who to himself is true, can ne'er be false to any other man." Truth to self means truth to our emotional, intel-

[marginal note: Apperception or Self-Consciousness.]

[marginal note: Conscience the Sense of God within us.]

lectual, and moral nature, or rather truth to *typical or ideal human nature.* **Only** from the reflective synthesis of these **can a** rational idea **of** Deity, and so of **duty,** be induced or inducted. This **induction from** experienced emotion, intellection, and pure **volition,** is **the** standpoint of transcendental or **sense-transcending** reason. The **idea of obligation, or duty,** obviously or **rationally refers to a person** other than **ourselves, that other person being the object of it, as** we are ourselves the **subject of it, a** relation having necessarily two terms —all duty **is to God,** whether that of proper self-regard, or of brotherly sympathy. The only rational idea of duty is what Jesus represented it to be, "Be ye perfect, as your Father in **heaven is per-**fect." That our Heavenly Father **or Creator has** Himself **attached a sense of peace or satisfaction to the fulfilment of, or obedience** to the **moral or** spiritual **order of His universe is obvious from the psychological fact** that "it is so" **with us.**[1] Even the observance of a merely mechanical or physical order has a strange attraction for human nature as such; but this last can **of** course degenerate **into our** becoming the slaves **of habit** and routine, **and making a** fetish of external **rules and** ceremonies, **of which** Jesus said, "The letter **killeth, but** the **spirit maketh alive."** Ceremonial **may become far-**cical, **when it is not the expression of real** feeling

---

[1] Just as Christians speak of the peace of God "that passeth understanding," the ancients spoke of the peace of the *mens sibi conscia recti.*

or real faith; but it is nonsensical, more than farcical nihilism, when it contradicts Self-consciousness in denying the validity of the fundamental necessary concepts of reason, such as the postulation of a Sufficient Cause, or one adequate to the production of a given effect, or that evolution involves involution, these being identical propositions.

If all energy were brought down to one uniform dead level of a common average, as the Socialist would have it, no further life, work, or emotion would exist.

It is Being *per se*, the one *Ding an sich*, which

Energy and Evolution are Individual.

is the object of all evolution; and Being is strictly individual. Inequality of individual endowment is the very source of the progress of societies, the higher status of the one constituting the present ideal of the lower individual or society. It is not a question of the quality or quantity of work accomplished by any one, but a question of WHAT *each man is himself, and is becoming*, so as to be fit for a nobler sphere in the life beyond the grave. "Everything," said Spinoza, "must be contemplated *sub specie æternitatis*."

"As it is by polar forces that the material world

"The Principle of Polarity" (Laing). The Dual Line or Law of Polarity; hence the Ineradicable Aspiration of Love.

is built up, so the principle of polarity manifests itself everywhere as the fundamental condition both of the material and spiritual universe" (Laing). Like attracting unlike, equally and oppositely in both kingdoms, definite structure always implying polarity. If attraction existed alone, all would come to a deadlock ; and if repulsion alone held sway, chaos would reign. For the play of electricity, one body must be negative to the other's positive.

" The law of polarity appears as a general law, under which, as the simple and absolute become differentiated by evolution into the complex and manifold, it does so *under the condition of developing contrasts*, which, although apparently antagonistic, it is only by their co-existence and mutual balance that harmony and order is possible " (Laing).

Herbert Spencer says : " As from the antagonistic social tendencies man's emotions always create, there always results, not a medium state, but a rhythm between opposite states—now the one greatly preponderating, and presently by reaction [the reaction of extremes] there comes a preponderance of the other. The one force or tendency is not a continuity unless counterbalanced by the other force or tendency." Perpetual motion is thus arrived at by sustained action and reaction, "equal and opposite." Hence the infinite variety, unstaled by custom, of true lovers' joys.

" As life develops from simpler into more complex forms, it does so under the law of developing *contrasts* or *opposite polarities*, which are necessary complements of each other's existence. As we ascend in the scale of life, we find existing the polarity of male and female" (Laing).

When two of opposite sex and complementary natures are united, great is the advantage they have over the single individual in the struggle for life. *La vie à deux est plus facile que la vie à un;* not as being duplicates, but as being supplements the one of the other; *contrapposto e compenso l'uno all' altro.* "The harmonious union of two highly-evolved personalities makes ideal perfection, but there must be identity or *equality of essence* (Entity or Being) developing itself in opposite directions for real suitability."

It is contrast that produces reaction, resulting in constant and most delectable and vivid surprises;

The Law of Contrast.

this is true love, "unstaled by custom." If the Ego, therefore, remains isolated from the closest of all intimacies, it sinks into a groove leading to the slough of doubt and despond. The union of our common mental activity, through which we *then* and *there* understand each other, is based on its essential connection with a common type of physical or neural organism. The union of the very high and very low types of humanity is infertile.

It is the give and take between two contrasted personalities, mutually or equally suited, that reveals, even to ourselves, our own best nature. When the disciples recognised Christ in the apparent stranger that walked with them from Emmaus, it was because of the glowing of their hearts within them, of their sympathy with Him. "In the union of a perfectly matched man and woman each finds in each *the explanation of their diversified being.*" Diversity of function does not prevent equivalence of being.

Count Leo Tolstoi says in his " Anna Karénine :"—
" Sa physionomie, calme et passive, semblait refléter
une âme élevée. Il la reconnut, et une joie illumina
son visage ; il ne pouvait s'y tromper : une seul
créature humaine *personifiait pour lui la lumière
de la vie.* Lá, dans cette voiture, qui s'éloignait,
était la réponse à l'énigme de l'existence qui l'avait
tourmenté si péniblement."

> "'Twas but a little while we loved ; then the whole world was
> our own ; "

for " the desire of our desires " is fulfilled, the means
to the end of joy of life is actualised.

Robert Browning sings in his last poem, as the fruit
of his matured years and wisdom—

> " All the **breath** and the bloom of the year **in the bag of one bee,**
> All the wonder and wealth of the mine in the heart of one gem,
> In the core of one pearl all the shade and the shine of the sea ;
> Breath and bloom, shade and shine—wonder, wealth, and, how
> far above them !
> Truth (abiding reality) that's brighter than gem,
> *Trust that's purer than pearl,*
> *Brightest truth, purest trust in the universe,* all were for me
> *In the kiss of one girl.*"—R. BROWNING.

This last line seems to " smack of bar-room ameni-
ties," but the limiting the kissing to one girl removes
it to the sphere of spiritual love, of which alone
fidelity can be predicated.

> "I am wrapt in blaze,
> Creation's lord, of heaven and earth
> Lord, whole and sole, by a minute's birth
> Through the *love in a girl.*"
>
> —R. BROWNING, *Asolando.*

" It is thyself, mine own self's better part ;
  Mine eye's clear eye, my dear heart's dearer heart ;
  My food, my fortune, and my sweet hope's aim ;
  My sole earth's heaven, and my heaven's claim."
                    —SHAKESPEARE, *Comedy of Errors.*

" M'appar sulla tomba qual sogno di speme,
  Quei giorni d'amor che vivemmo insieme."

Browning says, "No dreams are worth waking," because what God has prepared for us, far surpasses our wildest imaginings. " *Your resistless fact, leap of man's quickened heart.*" Once aware that your *regard claimed what his heart holds, woke,* as from its sward the flower passion, the dormant idea.

" The positive and negative principles," said Kung Lino, " influence, act upon, and regulate each other ;

Elective Affinities and Adaptations. hence loves and hates, and hence the intercourse of the sexes " (Chuang Tsu). Chuang Tsu says again, " Men value the phenomena of which the senses make them conscious, but not the *phenomena of the senses themselves.*" It is indeed strange that we should be struck with the beauty of flowers, with the strength and cunning of animals, and with the stupendousness of insensible nature, and yet fail to be struck with the wonderful adaptation of the external cosmos to *our sensitive organism,* and to the inner or spiritual world of reflective Beings, who are pleasurably, or painfully affected by all these things, and who are so constituted as instinctively to inquire concerning the origin and Author of these things as well as of their own existence. The *logical or scientific basis of love* and morality is the *constitution* **of** *man's mental or spiritual nature.* What *agrees with,* or satisfies this, is a due *relationship—one* **commensurate** *with reality.* Then we have the perfection of vitality— life in completeness. Then do life and the universe and its Creator seem *good* indeed, or actually to us, as producing the desired effect upon us, *i.e., the effect we have been made to anticipate.* Then do we yearn to bring the happiness of others up to the ideal standard to which we have ourselves attained, " having no more grudges in our hearts," as Mahomet promised his faithful.

As Sir John Lubbock remarks, " There can be no more ungracious saying than ' It is too good to be true !' " God's power of satisfying the creature He has created, far surpasses our own fancies. Eden is found again, wherever two complementary spirits have met and are united, so that the world cannot come in between them. With regard to the religious element in the ceremony of marriage, how can any two spirits enter into the rest and joy of perfect mutual love without kneeling in gratitude to the Father of Spirits and committing themselves and their happiness to the Giver of all perfect gifts ?

The law of polarity, or of opposite and equal attraction between spiritual complementaries, finds expression in the exclamation, " Sei, wie du bist, du bist mein all, in Zeit und Ewigkeit " (Whatever else thou art, my all in all art thou, both now and in eternity). " Du bist der

Spiritual Expression of the Law of Polarity.

Himmel mir bestimmt " ("Du Meine Seele " song—
Schumann). Hence the boundless satisfaction of true
love, which can never be realised in successive infi-
delities, only suited to the uncertain life of the lower
animals. Why did they love ? Because *he* was *he*,
and *she* was *she*.

Attractions are proportional to destinies. The
dove is not a fitting mate for the eagle. There must
be similarity of kind and equivalence of worth, for
suitability to exist. The person who feels no attrac-

Attractions.

tions, personal, scientific, or moral, plods
along the beaten track where he finds himself,
without even the ideal of *imitation* of similars ; *which
is the one ideal of the commonplace*, and thus isolated,
he lapses out of the social stratum in which he was
born, and falls lower and lower towards the level of
the dangerous or criminal classes. If a man be not
an original thinker, the least and the best he can do
is to follow suit with his peers. As a child imitates,
so do most of the commonplace.

To feel spiritual objective attraction is as natural
to man as to feel physical hunger and thirst ; but

**Objective
Spiritual
Attraction.**

whether we eat or we drink, or whatsoever
we do, we are bound to do all to the glory
of God ; that is to say, in obedience to the
reason with which He has distinguished us from the
lower animals, as considering whether the result of
our actions will be for the real best for Being—
the best for our spiritual or real Being—or a mere
momentary gratification through our senses. We

love, or are attracted by persons according to the relation of similarity, **equivalent** *correspondence*, **or** harmony, in **which they stand to us ; whilst if we** believe them **to** be antagonistic **to** us, or feel them to be deadening to our vitality or spiritual life, **we are** repelled **and shocked by them quite as much as if** they **attack** us with stones **or staves ; and if we give** ourselves up to such a feeling **without regard to** morality, we **are led to hate them**, *i.e.*, **to wish** their extinction, so that we may be **relieved** from the dis-tress they occasion us. Thus Christ said, " He who hateth his brother is a murderer." But hatred is not a feeling indulged in by the philosopher or wisdom-loving Being, knowing that *tout comprendre est tout pardonner*, and that a man is still **a fit subject for** benevolent **pity, whether** he **be friend or foe to us.**

It has been my ambition, **in** my work on " A New Theory of Idealism," to logically answer the ques-tions which have so much exercised the mind of the public of late, *i.e.*, 1st, " Is human life worth living?" 2nd, " Is marriage a failure ? "   3rd, "How is the battle of life to be conducted ? "   Strange to say, the fact of life being a struggle has been disputed **by** some in the late newspaper correspondence on these subjects, on the ground that they themselves enjoy *bicycling and like pretty scenery !* **as** the kitten licks its lips at the sight of milk.

The question as **to whether life** is worth living must logically be placed under the first principle of thought or **normal mental** representation, *i.e.*, **the** category of Sufficient Cause, which concerns the real nature of Being, or of Being as such ; so we have to ask, " What is the characteristic of man's nature specially ? " The second question comes under the second principle of thought, *i.e.*, that of Efficient Cause ; so the question stands, " In what relation does the conjugal object stand to the subject ? or how does marriage affect the destiny of man ? " Whilst the third question, " How is the battle of life to be conducted ? " comes under the third principle of thought, *i.e.*, that of Final Cause, and we find ourselves asking " What is the aim, end, or goal of man ? "

In order that the human intellect may be satisfied, or rest content in any essential judgment, these three modes of the intuitive representation of the modifications of the attributes or aspects of Being, viz., feeling, intelligence, and will, must be clearly understood and reflectively comprehended. For, in the first place, if any confusion be allowed to exist between our respective estimates of brute nature and of insect life, and that of human or spiritual Being, *no rational* solution of the question can be expected, seeing that the datum upon which all *reasoning*, inductive, or deductive, proceeds is the nature of personality, *i.e.*, of noumenal, self-conscious, or spiritual Being, as opposed to the mere phenomenal automatic existence of the lower animals. I use the word *automatic*, as opposed to *autonomous* self-direction. Also noumenal or spiritual Being is always

conceived of by us (again as *contrasted* with that
of the lower animals) through its enduring or per-
manent nature, although it may be temporarily
modified and conditioned in its activity in this
planet by what St. Paul called "this body of death,"
or by what has been scientifically denominated "a
sentient mechanism," adapted to carry out the life
of a finite being in this planet of Tellus.   Be it
observed that St. Paul looked to our being clothed
upon with a more glorious body in a future state of
existence.[1]   *Even here our material frame is inces-*
santly changing.   Thus, then, the first question ought
rather to be, " Is this telluric life worth living *to*
a spiritual being? "   And the answer which would
universally be given by reflective persons—such as
Shakespeare represents his Hamlet to have been—
is obviously, " *No*, certainly not," *as regarded per se,*
but also decidedly, " *Yes*, quite so," *when only re-*
garded as a preliminary school of training for another
and a better world.   Still it is only by those who
reverently and clearly grasp the principle, " *Qui*
veut la fin, veut les moyens," that it can be fully
and unhesitatingly accepted at each and every step
over what Sydney Smith called " the burning marl
of life."

With regard to the second question, " Is marriage
a failure ? " the answer to this logically depends upon

---

[1] We can even afford to grant Darwin's and Grant Allen's hypothesis,
that men were originally protected by a covering of hair, such as a
certain tribe in Japan have *now*.

the nature of the relation between the subject and the object concerned in it; and seeing that no two persons are exactly similar, and *that therefore only one can be a perfect match to another*, to be mated and not matched must needs be a failure. It is surely then not to be wondered at, that few marriages are a perfect success.

Now, what I have attempted to exhibit throughout my work on the ideals of the emotions, the intellect, and the will is, that the conjugal relation is an essentially correlative one. Given the *man*, the existence of the woman is also given, and *the converse;* human marriage being founded on the complemental nature of the two individual beings who enter into conjugal union. Amongst the lower animals it is enough that the sex is complementary.

It being a truism of psychological science that the subject is only logically revealed to itself through the object, which, by calling its faculties into play, as it were, *actualises* the subject; it is also true that only by the constant, continuous, complementary action and reaction of subject and object that the characteristically human powers of feeling, intelligence, and will are fully educed or evolved. Each idiosyncrasy requires by the term to be supplemented or complemented by its opposite, or other; so that what is wanting in the development of the one or the other as to the threefold attributes of personality, may be supplied and fortified by the spiritual and physical correlate.

Thus only can equilibrium be attained by finite creatures; and thus also it is only through the *joy-giving* union of counterparts that the reflective conception of the perfect goodness or perfection of the absolute Prototypal Being can be arrived at by any individual human being. For only thus is the perfect goodness or benevolence of God fully revealed to us. " Shall those in the pit praise Thee, O Lord ?" Is it out of the depths of spiritual isolation that the sweet incense of praise can arise ? Is not solitude, like despair, to a being so deeply and intimately social as man the destined social unit ?

Milton represents Adam standing between Eve and the Supreme Being, lest her sense of the Divine power should be too awful and too overwhelming to her to admit of her approach to the Father. Yet did not Dante describe *woman in the person* of *Beatrice* as drawing *man* first to *herself,* so as to teach him thus through perfect human love for the one nearer and dearer than all to love the invisible Father, and *recognise* His love for His spiritual offspring ? But if woman teaches man to love, man teaches woman justice : " **Fiat** justitia ruat cœlum,"—justice involving strength of intellect and will, which are more or less conditioned by physical strength.

Lastly, there remains the third question, Why is there such contention between our physical and our spiritual nature or interests ? And the answer is— Obviously because our spiritual evolution is conditioned and aided by that conflict. For matter can only be rationally regarded as subservient to, and as ministering to spirit, sensation being but the medium of emotional feeling. Thus the question, Why is life such a struggle? becomes rather, With what weapons is the battle of life to be fought? since fought it must be.

Now the answer to this remodelled question is that defensive weapons are the only ones needed, those namely, that are enumerated by St. Paul, and chief among these is the shield of faith, the one all-powerful weapon in life's warfare—faith in the Creator and Joy-Giver, which can only mean faith that all is for the best, that "all things are working together for good," and that we shall ultimately enter into *the joy of our Lord, which is the rest of love eternal;* and love is as the breastplate in the battle of life, so also only on the heart of love can the anchor of hope be struck. Love is at once the path and the goal; through it is the fulfilment of the moral laws. "As-tu de l'Idéal, mon frère? Ou, es-tu prêt à renoncer à ce que fut le rêve secret, l'espérance consolatrice de chacun de nous, même de ceux qui n'en ont jamais parlé?" Do you feel no sadness when happy lovers whisper to each other soft and low? Have you no faith in a Heavenly Father; no hope in His love, which, by the very nature of love, can but have benevolent ends in all the mysteries of His Providence? If not, what must have been your past, how devoid of love, "orphaned of the earthly love and heavenly," and what can your present lead you to expect in the future? No one can suffer without hope, who has once known the boundless tenderness of real love; but, alas! how can we be saved from doubt of what we have not ourselves experienced? For knowledge is but experience, our own, or that of others endorsed by our own positive, although it may be more limited, experience and reflective judgment.

As the external life is one of sensation, so the inner life is one of emotion, whether it be in the form of simple spontaneous spiritual attraction or that of reflective desire, both of which are accompanied by intellection of their causes, and by *the reflective drawing of conclusions as to consequences or necessary results from recognised causality.*[1] The facts of our vital experience in Being, and the fundamental principles of reason, which are correlate with these, constitute "the light of all our seeing;" self-cognition, whether intuitive or reflective, being the condition of all *recognition of similars*, as of all logical deliberate "*substitution of similars*" (Jevons).[2] To accept as realities the physical facts that fire burns and water drowns, *i.e.*, that both of these physical elements, although useful in many ways to man, can become dangerous or fatal to his physical life, leading to the rational conclusion that fire and water are good ser-

---

[1] Dr. Theodore Lipps calls these the "Grundthatsachen des Seelenlebens."

[2] The fundamental axiom of morals, "Do unto others as you would be done by," is a case of the "substitution of similars."

vants but bad masters, and then to ignore or deny
the facts of man's spiritual nature, or his intuitive
tendency to act for the conservation or true welfare
of Being, as such, is surely most irrational.   For
to lose sight of the fundamental law of self-con-
servation or self-reverence, is not only fatal to the
individual himself, but also harmful to all others in
different degrees, according to the different orders
and degrees of relationship in which a man stands
towards them ; for what measure would he then have
of their rational requirements of him?   If he like
to be down-trodden and despitefully used, he must
conclude that others like it also : again, seeing that
we can only predicate the goodness or benevolence
of God, from the existence of practical reason in ourselves, the unmindfulness of the moral nature of
man seems like madness. " I have been the friend
of all men," said a dying Persian king, mentioned
by one of the Greek historians, " why then should
I doubt that God will be my friend?"   And just
as it is folly to leave the physical senses uncul-
tured, so it is trebly folly not to endeavour to
train aright the spiritual faculties of faith, love, and
hope ; for to believe irrationally, to love irrationally,
and to hope irrationally, are fatal to man's best and
truest interests, both here and hereafter.   And as it
is now a postulate of psychical science that each thing
is seen by each person only through *the medium of his
own personal impressions, emotional and intellectual,
and from his consequent judgment therefrom,* which is

necessarily in accordance with the mode of thought
peculiar to each one's *idiosyncrasy* of representation, modified as the personality is by heredity and
subsequent external influences; great must be the
need of voluntary reflective self-culture, as well
as a good early education to assist us in feeling,
thinking, and acting rightly! "Nemo dat quod non
habet." We call a man who has no moral sense
"a good for nothing." What matters it how fast
or how commodiously we travel if it be not towards
the true goal of Being?[1] For actual evolution to take
place, no solitary self-culture will suffice. There
must exist the involuntary action and reaction of
one living spirit upon another, as steel must be struck
against flint for the spark of light to be produced, all
reflection being upon actual experience of feeling,
intelligence, and will. Thus true reflection on love,
can only come of related and mingled lives, and
only in the positive experience of bliss can the
certain hope of eternal blessedness that is caused
by the perfect joy of love arise in us in the second
birth of the Spirit, which can have no other root
but *faith in God* and in His unextinguishable goodness. All inference being from experience, had
perfect bliss never been experienced here, what pre-

---

[1] Mr. Grant Allen says : "If we can trust all that is reported of them,
ants have already reached the goal set before us as a delightful one by
socialist philosophers, in which the individual is absolutely sacrificed
in every way to the needs of the community." Now, as man differs
from ants in respect of introspective reflection, and the consequent
anticipation of a future and happier life, the rule of the ants cannot
be his.

F

dication could have been made concerning it for the future ?

When faith in God and His goodness wanes, so necessarily do also love and hope. "*Let us eat, drink, and be merry,*" that is all that then remains to be said. There is, however, a faint survival of our *ideal of beatitude* in the forlorn endeavour to be merry, when love and hope are gone. It is *only by being true* to the light of reflective reason, the light which "cometh down from the Father of lights," and through the practice that makes perfect, that we are enabled to draw unhesitating, broad, and general inferences as to the destiny of man *upon the reflective principle of Sufficient Reason, which is* furnished by the *introspective synthesis of the three categories of causality* presented in feeling, intelligence, and will, conditioned in their exhibition by the nervous or physiological system. These are *positive data*, which contain their own conclusions. The phenomena of our own consciousness compel us to ask for a cause, and, says Dr. Flint : " If we could once admit that there be anything" (I do not say any Being) "uncaused, there is no reason to assume a cause for anything." Power of feeling, and of inspiring feeling—Egoity—intelligence of relativity, and *consequent sympathies*—altruity—and religious practice, *i.e.*, action according to the order of pure Being, as established by the Deity in rational Being—morality —are the three essential elements of Being—the primordial sources of the principles of our understand ing, or of the categories of mental representation. As our vital experience *determines the forms of our spontaneous mental representations, so do the reflectively considered forms of thought categorise our experiences under the cosmic order of Sufficient, Efficient, and Final Causation.* Mental facts are determined by the order of a certain set of physical processes, *i.e.*, the physiological conditions on which sensation depends.

The basis of logic is metaphysical or ontological, and the reflective sciences of morality and theology are introspectively arrived at through reflection on the *Subject-Object*, which involves *recognition of First and Final Causality*. Herbert Spencer says : " We cannot carry on an inquiry concerning Causation without inevitably committing ourselves to the hypothesis of a First Absolute Cause." Thus " the logical formulæ are the predicates of God " (Hegel). For it is by introspective observations of the *modifications* of our own Being, through the affections of our nervous system, that we trace the genesis of the fundamental ideas of reason in our own emotional, intellectual, and moral states. But alas ! whilst we are clad in " this vile body," accidental and hereditary deteriorations of the nervous system often trouble and confuse normal mental representation, and the sweet bells jangle out of tune when Reason ceases to hold her sway ; hypnotised patients are also instances of this suppressed *self*-consciousness.

No definition of anything can proceed upon negatives. Joy, which is the positive sense of Being, is more positively instructive than sorrow. Even to conceive negation there must be positive conception of some reality. Suffering itself is caused in us by the negation of the joy of life we *need* so much, and therefore *rationally expect.* Unreality is the absence of truth, lovelessness the absence of harmony, injustice the absence of goodness.

The type, or ideal of Being, of which our understanding consists, is characterised by feeling, intelligence, and moral will ; will for the conservation of Being, as opposed to the evil, or defective will, which seeks the lesion and destruction of Being ; as the fox of Æsop's fable, which, having lost its own tail, recommended all other foxes to cut off theirs. " We define life outside ourselves, only as we know it in ourselves, as a striving after good " (Tolstoi). By *good* we understand the best, the *summum bonum.*

An individual, or person, wanting in any one of the three normal aspects, or manifestations of Being, is as much a monster in the spiritual world, as a calf with two heads or three legs is in the physical world ; only that spiritual monstrosity is far more dreadful, as it is farther-reaching in its consequences to others. " If each man did not desire his own happiness separately, he could not perceive anything separately, could never have understood anything living " (Tolstoi).

To be without feeling is to be without the primary foundation of morality ; and to be without intelligence of causality also renders true morality impossible.

The internal bond of cause and effect, is only known to man through his rational reflective self-consciousness. The external bond between **cause and effect,** is merely that of Efficient Causation, which **treats only** of the relation between things — not of their Sufficient, **nor of their Final** Cause, but only of their action and reaction upon one another.

Science is of the special—*la philosophie envisage le tout.* Hence the name given to those who devote themselves to its study, viz., **lovers of** wisdom, **of** understanding, of ideal knowledge **for** its own sake.

One class of mind, that of the scientist, desires above all to know the exact truth upon some particular subject; another class, that of the poet **or** artist, *par excellence,* aspires to grasp the **har-monious or** beautiful, both in physical **and spiritual** nature. The poet, as Browning says, teaches "**the music of man and maid;**" whilst the third representative class of humanity is bent upon carrying out practically the **good or best** for Being—such are the moralists and philanthropists.

Each of these three classes, in order to be *power-fully effective,* or *completely representative men,* must look through nature and **human** nature up to Nature's God, whose Being is the Ideal or Pattern of all excellence, Who is the true Living Source of real Ideality; **for it is in** giving **man** the reflective sense of Ideal Being, **that** God has revealed Himself to him, and **marked** him with His seal or effigy **as the crown** of creation. Spiritual Being is **the test of all truth,** all beauty, all rightness; only in relation to real Being can we conceive anything. " Only after having fixed upon an immovable point as a centre, can a region or surrounding district be described. Having reflectively realised in what my happiness (or *bien-être*) consists, I shall be in a condition to recognise in what consist the life and happiness of other beings. But the happiness or life of other beings, I cannot in any way know without having acknowledged my own. Observations upon other beings striving towards the aims which were unknown to me, constituting *semblances* of that happiness, the striving after which, I *know* in myself, can explain nothing to me, but can certainly hide from me my true knowledge of life. Hence observation begins when life is already known. Without a confession that this striving after good which man feels within himself is life, and an image of all life, no study of life is possible, and no observation of life is practicable. I know that the claim of each Being is his own happiness, because I know myself as an individual striving after happiness"—*re*-cognition being of the cognised (Appendix to " Life "—Tolstoi).

Reflective obedience to the moral law lies in leaving no part or attribute of human nature completely undeveloped, herein lies the true ministry of education and the duty of subsequent self-culture.

Nevertheless, from the very force of the Divine law or order of idiosyncrasy, no finite Being standing alone is perfectly equilibriated, or has perfectly-balanced faculties, but rather is chronically in the state of defective equilibrium, which of itself tends to error, evil, and distress. Such spirits are " wandering shapeless flames," not representing Being in its integrity as a perfect circle, full-orbed. " A bachelor !" exclaims Grant Allen, " self-centred ! the root of all evil, if people would but see it !"

But as in physical nature, one law is often met by the counterbalancing influence of another law, so in spiritual nature the law of idiosyncrasy has its counterbalancing influence in that of sex. Male and female created He humanity ; the balance that cannot exist in the finite individual, has been divinely furnished by the union of the two complementary natures. "Marriage involves the highest ideal, for the well-assorted union of the two in one, gives a more complete equilibrium and reconciliation of opposites, than can be attained by the single individual, who must always remain more or less within the sphere *of the polarity* of his, or her respective sex" (Laing), " harmony or perfection depending on the due balance of the opposite qualities " (Ibid.) ; an identity or equality of essence with development in different directions, presenting the state of mobile equilibrium which is at once more free, and more enduring than any condition of stable equilibrium could possibly be.

Now whilst these positive realities of our Being assert themselves in us, it is simply ludicrous to flourish the banner of Agnosticism, or nonsensical nescience, regarding Being, and the relativity of

Being, or the tendency of Being to seek the best for Being. To pretend to delight in toil and trouble without a happy end in view is, as though one should assert that the black shadow was the reality, instead of the sun or light-dispensing substance. For love, or the sense of spiritual relativity, answers in the spiritual sphere to light or motion in the material world, just as obtusity, or absence of feeling answers to density and darkness. Where love, the light of life and of the heart, reigns supreme, "the shadow on the dial only proves the presence of the sun," but where love is not, the soul is shrouded in a darkness "that can be felt."

I was once shown into a room lighted wholly by luminiferous or phosphoric paper, and the one thing there that struck me, besides the sad subduedness of the light, was the utter absence of shadow. This reminded me of the fool's paradise, whose denizens move in a like ghostly or unreal atmosphere of so-called gaiety, or make-believe of joy, feeling nothing deeply or truly, and therefore proclaiming that life has no shadows in it. Of course, if we never go up, there is certainly no fear of our ever going down, and he, who knows not real joy, can scarce know sorrow. Certain it is, also, that without a substance being present to reflect, refract, or absorb the sun's rays, there can be no shadow thrown; yet he who mistakes the shadow, which answers to doubt in the intellectual world, for the real substance of thought, is truly most pitiable. George Eliot remarked that

" it is strange how little pity is felt for wrong ideas, they being the sources of so much evil."

It is from existence and not from *non*-existence that we argue. Yet a positively felt need within us, say of physical food, *suggests* to us, through our intelligence of relativity or efficient causation, that something must exist having efficiency of affinity with our constitution, to build up and support our physical organism. In like manner, when suffering from spiritual loneliness, and the depressed vitality that the sense of forlornness brings with it, and comparing our then sad state of Being to the cheerfulness we experience when with congenial, and therefore sympathetic, fellow - creatures, and above all, with our soul's delight, our best beloved, we argue that our spiritual requirement is emphatically that of sympathy. Accordingly, in order to lessen, or do away with the dissatisfaction with which we regard life in isolation, we seek friendly companionship— the next best thing to " Love," " the Lord of all," who comes *un*sought, *un*bought, a monarch to His own. For the sense of loneliness is never truly extinguished; the need of a closer and more intimate communion ever remains in us, as a sad sense of unappeased longing, until our soul's true correlate appears. Tennyson, in one of his latest poems, " Happy, or the Leper's Bride," says :—

The Restful Sense of Soul-Completion.

" In the name of the everlasting God, I will live and die with you.
This wall of solid flesh, that comes between your soul and mine,
Will vanish, and give place to the beauty that endures—
The beauty that endures on the spiritual height,

> When we shall stand transfigured, like Christ on Hermon hill,
> And moving each to music, soul in soul and light in light,
> Shall flash through one another in a moment, as we will.
> If you be dead, then I am dead, who only live for you.
> . . . . I hear a death-bed angel whisper 'Hope.'
> The miserable have no medicine, but only hope."

Swedenborg taught that the just, even dead or passed beyond this world, cannot realise the full blessedness of heaven until they have each their mate. Patience is involved in rational hope together with the converse. There is an order in self-fulfilment. The fruit plucked too early is immature. *Tout vient à point à qui sait attendre.* "Mitra Nirvana, Nirvana of my eyes, still I walk in dreams. For that time, though past, *still* lives for me—*that alone is the reality in which I live;* waking existence where *that* is not, is but a pale dream. The clouds which veiled *the future, and us* from each other were pierced in a moment when, in a lightning-flash, we found that *we were what we had been searching for* through life and the world" (Sanskrit poem).

> "No second morn has ever shone for me,
>   All my life's bliss is in the grave with thee;
>   Once having drunk of that divinest gladness,
>   How could I face the empty world again?"

> "Soul of my soul! supreme and strong,
>   Together we can do no wrong—
>   Apart, no right."

"My life is blessed with thoughts of thee for ever and for ever."

"His image persisted through everything as a vague background of her consciousness. Henceforward a part of her life, a factor in her life's history" (Grant Allen).

The universe is rationally conceived as the habitat of Being. "The ideas of reason give *unity* to our multifarious cognitions." "Reason sets a man upon that sole path which opens ^{Justice and Virtue.} to him afar off the indubitable immortality of life, and its happiness" (Tolstoi). We recognise the Divine ideas in the universe for the sufficient reason that we reflectively cognise our own. Through reflection is *self-possession,* in which human dignity consists. We must first know ourselves, to be able to be true to ourselves, and only by being true to ourselves can we fulfil the functions for which we are designed. Justice is the result of the complementary action of the three faculties of the soul, each faculty keeping its own place in executing its appointed function. According to Plato, justice lies in the *equipoise of the different principles of our nature.* "The true nature of a thing is [Individuality.] another word for its virtue." When the virtue, or essence, of a perfume is exhausted, we throw it away. "Disease is in the soul when any of its parts do not conform to the nature of the whole. We must be rational if we would be *men*" (Ferrier). To be irrational is to be less than man. "If rational consciousness does not drive a man, with his will, or against it, to the only true path of life, then the suffering which flows from error will so drive him." The good is the perfection of our nature; the desire for the good is our common point of agreement; but we are mostly ignorant of wherein it truly lies.

Thought and reason cannot be separated from self-consciousness. " Without the knowledge of myself as separate from everything else, **I** should know nothing of any other life." "Generalisation of re-flective reason is always of the facts of *individual experience.*" " Thy life is my life, with its aspirations for happiness, but it is also an illustration of similar Beings, if **I** am normally constituted." " **A** man must believe in his wings, and soar where they bear him " (Tolstoi).

" Men, as one rational whole, are driving towards the same happiness." " The Ego which reflects, is as a cord, on which the various consciousnesses which follow each other in point of time are strung." Can I regard this rational consciousness as only a reflec-tion of something unnecessary, and superfluous ? That in which the consciousness of the true life of man resides, is not affected by time, or space, or by temporary lapses of terrestrial consciousness.

" More powerfully and convincingly than through either reason or history, and from quite a *different source, as it were, does the aspiration of man's heart reveal itself* to him, *impelling* him to *immediate* happiness, to that very activity which his reason has pointed out to him, and which is expressed in his heart *by love* " (Tolstoi). " There are wants of our real life, as well as of our animal personality. In the satisfaction of the mere conditions of existence, the wants of our true life must not be forgotten." " When we devote all our mind to a recognised

animal want, animal desires rule us, hiding from us
our true wants as human beings." "The weeds of
our thickly-grown vices have stifled the germs of
true life in us." "What is required is not *renuncia-
tion of individuality, but its subjection to rational
consciousness*" ("Life," p. 153, Tolstoi). "It is
neither possible nor necessary to renounce individuality, and a man may, and ought, to make *use of the
given conditions* of life, but he must not look upon
these conditions as the end and aim of life. All
men know from the earliest years of their childhood
that, in addition to the happiness of the animal person, there is another and better happiness of life.
Not a something or other that must be sought somewhere, that is promised at some time, but the happiness which is familiar *to man in the feeling of Love*"
(Tolstoi).

"Love is the only reasonable activity of man."
"Love is the sole legitimate manifestation
of *rational* life. Love is activity, directed
to the good for Being." "If a man decide
that it is better for him to refrain from the demands
of the smallest present love in the name of a future
and deferred manifestation of love, then he deceives
either himself or others, and loves no one, but himself alone." (Only he who is faithful in little will
be faithful in much.) "The possibility of true love
begins only when a man has comprehended that the
satisfaction of his animality is not happiness; only
then will all the sap of his life pass into the one

*Love alone
confers
Happiness
upon Man.*

ennobling shoot of genuine love. People who do not know what real life is, call merely existing living." Lust is not love. " The various carnal desires of man are but weeds resembling love. Men even prefer at first these weeds, which stifle the one shoot of real life, which they trample down, and begin to *rear another shoot from the weeds,* calling it love. Then the same men, or others, say, ' All this is non-sense, folly, sentimentality.' Love needs but one thing, that men *should not hide from it the sun of reason,* which alone will promote its growth. How long will men continue to gratify the desires of this perishing existence, and thereby deprive themselves of *the possibility* of the only happiness in life— Love ?"   " The mood of love presents itself to those who do not understand life, not as an essential point in human life, but as an *accidental* frame of mind. Whereas it is love that gives the greatest possible happiness to man, thus solving all the contradic-tions of life."   Like a key made for this one lock alone, man finds in his *own soul a feeling* which not only solves the contradictions of life, but finds in these very contradictions a possibility of manifesting itself (" Life," p. 166, Tolstoi).

There is *no happiness different from or opposed to virtue.*   " The *good is the supreme category of the universe."*   " *True Being and the good are iden-tical."*   " Love, as the *source of joy* and the ful-filment of the law, is the conciliation of virtue and happiness." Love is the source of all energy. Tolstoi says, "Ce qu'il nous importe de savoir, c'est le but de la vie et notre place dans l'ensemble des choses." *It is love in all its degrees that reveals this to us.*

It is Thought which brings the mind into relation with the Supreme Being.[1] The Pyrrhonic scepticism was founded on the relativity of all knowledge to the individual thinker, but this was **Thought.** not, in fact a *rational* ground for doubt. "*Quicquid recipitur, recipitur ad modum recipientis.*" "The life *contrary to nature and reason is wrong, because it makes us miss the designed end.*" "*Happiness is the end for which all beings live.*" The life *according to the spirit is the life natural to man,* as distinguished from the brute. "*Homo mensura.*" Man being the *measure,* we regard or judge of everything in relation to him. A Sufficient Cause and a Final Cause always imply intelligence; hence resentment is felt at a vicious will. "*Feeling is the essential constituent of happiness. Our thirst for knowledge, love, and goodness being appeased, we are happy, content, or satisfied.*" "Nous ne souffrons alors plus de la nostalgie du bonheur." We no longer ask, "What is the meaning of life?" or "Is life worth living?" Plotinus recommended *self-reflection,* or the study of our thoughts, as the highest duty. "*All instances are instances of something—the something is an idea of reason.*" "Our whole know-

---

[1] "Thoughts are the inchoate but plastic material of Theology. Theology cannot be divorced from its root in the spirit and conscience of man."

ledge of outward things is based entirely on our ideas " (Ferrier). " Ideas are elicited into consciousness *on the occasion of some outward impression, or some impression on the imagination.*" " Self-consciousness exhausts the meaning of the universe as an object of thought or possible mental representation." " The principles of reason are as universal as *Being is naturally conceived to be.*"

Morality means practice or action *according to Being;* consequently the ultimate ratio of man's duty

Duty and Happiness. is Egoity, Altruity or Sympathy, and theopathy. "Love thy neighbour *as thyself,* and adore the Lord thy God with all thy powers of feeling, intelligence, and will," was Christ's estimate of human duty. " L'amour est l'ultima ratio de toutes choses." " Nothing is so inspiring, nothing so restraining, as love." Aristotle says, " It is not difficult to see the *identity of essence and end.*" *Evolution is from potentiality to actuality of Being.* " *God is the Eternal Self-thinking Reason*" (Aristotle). " All subordinate ends are means to the chief good." Love, or spiritual harmony, is the goal of evolution, the *summum bonum,* beatification. Man's true enjoyment lies in the exercise of his faculties, and, as *Aristotle says, " in the midst of favourable external conditions.*" " *The action of reason upon passion is the field of morality*" (Aristotle). " The happiness of any being must be intimately connected with the functions it has to discharge." The Stoics taught that man has *first to conform himself to the* *law of his own nature ; secondly, to the law of society ; and thirdly, to the law of* **Providence,** *answering to self - love, social, and divine,* meaning an entire voluntary compliance with, as well as submission to, the will of the **Creator.** The temper of mind which constitutes **virtue is threefold,** *i.e.,* **right feeling, right thinking, and right action,** or self-determination according to Reason. " *The Stoical apathy meant freedom from perturbation, not from passion controlled by reason.*"

When Kant shocked the world by adding to his statement of the existence of definite, necessary, or natural forms of thought the *nota - bene* that " *because we are compelled to repre-* Of the Categories of Thought. *sent things to ourselves under* **these forms** *or categories of the understanding,* that is no proof that they correspond with reality," he broached a sophistry more astounding than had ever been heard before, seeing that we unhesitatingly proceed in all our actions upon the principle of *Sufficient* **Reason** *adducing the trustworthiness of our external and internal senses, for* **whatever we** *believe,* **feel, and do** (*to be, to suffer, and to do* constituting **our** *grammatical formula of consciousness*), seeing *that* **we produce** *the effects* **we desire from so** *trusting* **to our senses** *corrected by our reason.* How, then, can **we pretend** to question the validity of that same Reason ? If, as we are now told by M. Taine and Compagnie, we may not trust the *reality* of our own Being, it follows, of course, that we cannot trust the representations of Being, or of its elements : feeling, intelligence, and will, of which our consciousness consists. But seeing that these very doctrinaires feed their bodies, and carry their intelligence and wills into effect, *i.e.*, show themselves to be sufficient causes by the effects they produce, their nihilistic dogmas naturally appear nonsensical to us, and our faith in Being, our own, and theirs, remains unshaken, although doubt, scepticism, or cynicism, may be their mode of expressing themselves.

The mind proceeds according to the same method in apperception or reflective contemplation of the Subject-Object as it does in spontaneous perception in postulating Sufficient, Efficient, and Final Causality, and thus logically predicating an Intellectual, *Absolute*, and Benevolent Cause, as the rational explanation of our own *relative* and moral Being, an infinite origin for the manifold of finite sentient beings, who is also the Creator and adapter of the physical conditions under which they live and move and have their Being. To what, or rather to whom, are we to attribute our endowment of a moral sense or benevolent purpose in action, if not to a Being who is Himself benevolence or love, as well as power, and wisdom, seeing that our reason has its only standing-place, or starting-point for inference, in our *own Being* or *experience* in Being? Is it not the flat contradiction of reason to pretend to believe that order exists without an intelligent, benevolent Ordainer of Order, seeing what disorder

our own affairs fall into when we do not bring
intelligence to bear on them, or when *that order has
not benevolent purpose for its end*, which we know
to be the idea of typical Being. Well-Being is un-
deniably the aim of our own will, and it is this
intuition of reason, springing from the psychological
fact of our own instinctive action for the conservation
and delectation of Being, and our rational induction
therefrom, which alone enables us to predicate the
good-will of our Creator, on the principle of the logical
substitution of a similar cause for a similar effect.
" Through your own fatherhood read God's heart."

" Although the *self* is usually not a prominent or
explicit portion of a direct perception, yet when we
see a tree, a brain is implicit, a retina is implicit, and
the act of *seeing by a subject is implied*." Even *for
the representation of the past, the present*   Tests of
self is present in clear ideation. " The idea   Truth.
I *is interchangeable with that of force or cause*, as
also *with that of intelligent or Sufficient Causation*."
The one test of truth is, " *Do* our conclusions work?"
as the test of our faith is, "*Do we act upon it?*"
Another test of truth is, "Does *it fit in with other
knowledge positively* possessed by us?" How do we
know anything of the laws of Nature except through
the experience of mankind? " We have faith in
facts;" thus we have faith in causality through our
being able to produce effects, and through our being
equally affected by other objects. Power is the
necessary consistent outcome of *Being*. Knowledge

is the elaboration of the data *yielded by the nature of things.* " Action, proper or intelligent, is reaction to an external or an internal stimulus." Co-existence with another soul may induce cravings *undreamt of by the Subject-Object when alone.*" Love makes a man desire so to act that it may be well with all. "Only in loving is the spirit truly alive." " The internal state of one being in sympathy and harmony with another possesses a *radiatory* force, *resulting in another state of that other* being." Love is the most joyful activity of life. *Reflective reason represents our own modes of causality.* The combined dual reflection of complementary beings affords necessarily a *more complete image or archetype of human nature* than does that of a *lop-sided or idiosyncratic development.* " The sequences of observed cause and effect are Nature's promises ;" and when they seem to fail, our intelligence fails also. "*Always*" is our expression of the trustworthiness of cause and effect, as also of the logical principle of Identity and of the uniformity of Nature. Our *primitive representations* are those of the imagination, *when reason has operated upon* these, *they pass into knowledge.* " One man can only enter into the spirit of another through sympathy." " To regard God as a being like ourselves may be called noumorphic ;" but is not all spiritual *re*-cognition a perception of similarity or apprehension of noumenal relativity, and hence equally noumorphic ? Although it is through our own physical frame that we *re-*

cognise our own kind *directly*, it is through our own spiritual Being that we recognise the Father of Spirits *indirectly*, and logically, through the *reflective* "substitution of similars."

The laws of our spiritual nature, as well as those of our physical nature, have to be attended to and respected. We hear a great deal about unhealthy bodies, but the word *insanity* **Laws.** or *unhealthiness of mind* is only used in very extreme cases. To have a right to pass judgment on others, one ought to have, and be *true to*, a high intellectual and moral standard. A complementary, sympathetically-united pair *can better withstand being acted upon from without* by trying and painful circumstances than can the solitary mind convulsed with unbalanced emotions. The *bliss of a satisfying spiritual union is of itself a tonic* bracing us for the battle of life. " The reaction of one thing upon another is the consistent result of its own specific nature " (Lotze).

> " Thus both do fasten upon what's the main,
> And so their life and vigour do maintain."

" *A universal system of law unites* together all beings and *regulates their mutual* communication" (Lotze). " The state of one element contains a call to the other to change its condition if one is to be affected by the other " (Ibid.). " The function of philosophy is the clearing up of conceptions." " Ce qu'il nous faut ce sont des idées claires " (Descartes). " *Æsthetical, intellectual, and moral ideals* represent judgments according to abstract universal laws. " We are forced to conceive of an Infinite Being, of whom all finite beings are the cherished outcome." "*Reciprocation of internal states can only proceed from a vital mutual relationship, derived from the common substance from which they spring.*"   " I should have loved thee less, loved I not virtue (*i.e.,* obedience to the Creator) more."

A relationship consisting of two factors, one of which cannot be mentioned without implying the existence of the other, is termed a *corre-*

Correlations.

lation. By the expression " son," a father is understood, or necessarily represented in thought ; by that of " husband," a wife, and so forth. *Each finds in each the explanation of each other.* The completion of humanity, presented in the union of man and woman, cannot be singly represented *logically or ideally* by one of either sex. It is in their correlation that the rational representation of Being, and therefore of the *Ideal Being,* is rendered possible. A *rational* creature can *rationally* trust in the existence of Him who has so constituted our understanding that to know ourselves to be created is equally to know that our Creator must exist. " Self-consciousness is the category through which we think everything else. It is the category that determines existence, that is the most adequate to determine it."   Once having arrived at the conception of God through reflective reason, it follows, of course, as St. Paul says, that the knowledge of God and of the life eternal are identical, it being the only conceivable justification of all our sufferings here.

"Self-verification, or self-evidence, is the ultimate appeal of reason." Where will you find a man so all-sided that he can build out of his own consciousness, or reflection, or research, a symmetrical idea of the Divine nature which has all the elements of Being in proportion and balance? There are causes more than your volition by which you are governed. "Your *inherited* organic nature, its hungers and its attractions, will fulfil your destiny in spite of you, and *over you, as well as through you: hence the need of a counter-check*" (H. W. Beecher). "The man's mind seeks that which shall feed its strongest faculties, and, drawing out these elements, he leaves all others. For men's minds are magnets, and each one's magnet *draws those things for which there is attraction for him individually.*"

"Love," says Coleridge, "*is the sense of the insufficiency of the Self for the Self.*"[1] Love is an

---

[1] Sir John Lubbock says, in second part of "The Pleasures of Life," "The origin of love has exercised philosophers almost as much as the origin of evil," and he proceeds to quote Aristophanes, who says, "The making one of two is the healing of the state of man, and when the one finds his other half, the pair are lost in *amazement* of love and intimacy, and one will not be out of the other's sight, as I may say, even for a minute. They will pass their whole lives together, yet they could not explain what they desire of one another; for the intense yearning which each of them has toward the other, does *not* appear to be the desire of lovers' intercourse, *but of something else* which *the soul* of either evidently *desires*, but of which she has only an obscure and doubtful presentiment." Now, it has been my chief object in all my works to explain or give the rationale of this desire, as being the yearning for fulness or completeness, or equilibrium of Being.

activity which has for its end and aim happiness. Happiness is the reward of love. As chemical affinities assert themselves, so also do spiritual affinities (*Wahlverwandschaften*). Therefore life is a desert, when uncheered by human love and unsupported by religion, or Divine love. Were it not for some one, whom it would be possible to eternally love, what would a future state be? "Love is a beneficial activity, giving happiness to the person loved and to the one who loves."

The peculiar combination of essential qualities which has drawn two souls to each other here, will necessarily attract them to each other for ever, and everywhere, so that if the memories peculiar to earth fail them, their individual entity will still be recognised : at all events, each will *recognise their joy-giver* under their Creator's law, or according to His design. The physical conditioning of the order of their several generation is probably *the occasion* of their idiosyncratic development ; but who shall declare the generation of finite individuality any more than comprehend Infinite Personality? What we do know is, that in reflective reason, " man has wings to soar, without which he never would have mounted on high, and would not have beheld the abyss." But man must be born again to the Spirit for true love, faith, and hope to be possible to him ; for faith must be spiritual, love must be spiritual, and hope must be spiritual.

Meanwhile the existence of the fact of idiosyncrasy

Essential Qualities.

is unassailable, and the requirement of each of the complementary spirits for each other, and their consequent mutual attraction, is an equally indisputable fact. Only what gives to each of us fulness or the sense of completeness of Being, can communicate to us perfect joy of life for evermore in the presence of an approving Creator, who thus, His design being accomplished through the happiness of His rational creatures, sees that " His work is good." And can we doubt the rational assurances of St. John's revelation that God has prepared a rest (Nirwana) or state of blessedness for all who in due time arrive at understanding His law, and act in loving obedience to Him—an everlasting habitation, where " there shall be no more death, neither sorrow nor crying, neither shall there be any more pain"? As Jesus said, " What man is there of you whom, if his son ask bread, will give him a stone? How much more, then, shall your Father which is in heaven give good things to them that ask Him?" Surely the all-wise, all-powerful, and all-benevolent Father has in store for us a "house beautiful," amid His many mansions in the skies, where the "fitness of things" (taught by Cudworth and his school) will be fulfilled or revealed. " The ultimate fact of knowledge is neither pure Object nor pure Subject." [1] " although the world is intelligised through the Self, and intelligised by

---

[1] The doctrine of Protagoras was not a pure Subjectivism, but "an objective and realistic Relativism." "Hegelian or Rosminian Idealism is extremely realistic."

the Self." Philosophy, with its subsidiary sciences, is but the interpreter of the facts of human experience. Reason only represents the modifications of Being.

We see in the history of the Reformation that that great movement could not have taken place by the quiet influence of a sober, studious Melancthon alone; it required also the burning energy of a fiery Luther to spread the doctrine like a conflagration. Giordano Bruno says, "To inflame others we must ourselves be inflamed." Thus also without our counterpartal opposite we are weak and helpless, because we only take a one-sided view of life, and of our relations to other beings, whom our complementary spirit helps us to understand. A one-sided judgment is a half-truth: a sound judgment involving the equal action of all the intuitions of truth. Some may be found to say that they are quite happy without a complementary, or guardian, spirit. Thus also we were assured that many of the Negro slaves were happy in their slavery. In fact, it requires evolution of feeling and of ideality to perceive that we are *not* happy. "L'être prend sa place au monde selon sa capacité de souffrir du manque de l'Idéal." I will at least be bold to say that, without the many-sided capacity resulting from the union of complementary souls for sympathy, they are not so likely to make others happy.

As the final rational source or cause of activity is the instinctive pursuit of the good for Being, which is, reflectively viewed, the endeavour after its highest and best realisation, so the efficacious means to this end is love or harmony with typical or spiritual beings, and above all, with the Prototypal Being. The good for Being is only attained through self-love, social, and divine, or say self-reverence, social regard, and adoration of the Divine Will or of the Supreme Being—love having been defined by Spinoza as *joy caused by another being.*

It has been truly said that the word *goodness* applies to the end or final cause of action, and that of *rightness* to the means to that end. Final Cause, The pursuit of the best for Being is *in-* Conscious Content of *stinctive, necessitated, fatal;* our choice *lies* Being. *in the selection of the means* to it. Kant called metaphysics the science of *à priori* conceptions. Metaphysical notions accordingly are true, even if not (at once) " confirmed by practical experience." Thus it is with the " ought to be " of ethics, and with man's rational forecast of ultimate beatitude.

Locke, speaking of evidence, says : " The evidence is as great as we can desire, being as certain to us as our pleasure and pain, *i.e., happiness or misery, beyond which we have no concernment, either of knowledge or being.*" Such an assurance of the existence of things without us is sufficient to direct us in the attaining of the good, and avoiding the evil, which is caused by them, which is the important concernment we have in being made acquainted with them.

To quote Professor W. James : " Only what stirs us is realised. The question is, what does this stirring, this exciting power, this *interest* consist in, which some objects have? *Which are those intimate relations with our life which give reality to it?*" "The whole history of human thought is but an unfinished attempt to answer these questions. For *what* have men been trying to find out, since men were men, *but just these things: Where do our true interests lie? Which relations shall we call the intimate and real ones?* Which things shall we call *living realities,* and which not?"

These are the questions treated of alike in each of my three works. Many writers have expounded scientific truths logically, and also ethical verities; whereas the imaginative descriptions of the poets have seemed hitherto to suffice as a notice of the supreme form of both physical and spiritual attraction, which is *emphatically* called *love;* but seeing that it is the one relation, or rather correlation, in which both present and eternal felicity is concerned, seeing that through this nearest and dearest of relations, two solitary, and so forlorn, individualities are built up into the "strong, beautiful, and free" social unit— strong through the union of complementary characteristics, beautiful because of their harmony, and free from all grudges, envyings, and malevolence, by reason of their own perfect happiness or perfection of Being and grateful adoration of the Supreme Being, it has not seemed to me to be a superfluous endeavour to strive to give to conjugal love (meaning thereby what Shakespeare calls "the true marriage of souls") its real place in the essential interests, being, and destiny of man.

As Milton says, we need not despair of the high bidding of the Eternal being accomplished, whether any of us fall vanquished in "the fight of life for light," or not. It is a question of "what profiteth our own soul." St. Paul says: If a man give his body to be burned and all his goods to the poor, and hath not charity, what profiteth it his own soul? And again it may be said: Though a man, through sustained mental application, may invent a steam-engine or a telephone, what shall it profit his own soul on the day of moral reckoning? For this is man's real ground of responsibility to his Maker. In spite of the jeerings to which Christians have been exposed on the subject of seeking their own salvation, the Father of the universe, like an earthly parent, is rationally supposed to hold dear the blessedness of each of His children, and, like an earthly parent, He wills not that they should be careless of it; neither doth He "willingly afflict them." He does not afflict them for the pleasure of seeing them broken with anguish and sick with "hope deferred." His chastenings are but to fit us all for ultimate happiness, seeing that for the disobedient, the unjust, the disorderly, the malevolent, *happiness is impossible* and unattainable until evil ways are *repented of*, and goodness is pursued both for its own beautiful sake and because of its being the law of the Creator that we should do so. Salvation is from lovelessness to love or joy of being, from ignorance to knowledge of causes, from injustice or cruelty to goodness or benevolence.

It is to the spiritual obverse, or spiritual *impression made upon us* by another's personality, that

Spiritual Impressions. heed must be given in making a judgment of character. The hard-hearted will always leave us chilled, in spite of the fine sentiments they may politely parrot; the inane, after all said, and done, will leave no satisfactory impression upon our intellect, and the lawless, immoral nature will leave us with a scared sense of insecurity in our dealings with them, and alas! also with others. "We must take in the personal and concrete, as a direct immediate language, not a mediate language, or one which has to be translated into the notional or abstract before it means anything."

Still it is the typical attributes of Being which constitute the Ideal we are ever seeking to realise,

The Ideal. both objectively and subjectively; and well may those who never find them in their own familiar friends bewail the unreality of persons and nothingness of things. It is through the intuition of Ideal Being, "que nous demandons au monde le mot de son énigme," that which each one desires to realise.

> "L'Hymen sublime,
> L'Idylle éternelle."

> "Est ce pour le tombeau qu'un jour on nous fit naître?
> Et qui nous a menés à ce but effrayant?
> Est-ce donc pour cela que nous avons *tant aimé* ?
> Et longuement cherché le vrai, le beau, et le bien?
> *Et que tant d'Idéal en nous fut enfermè ?*"

St. Paul exclaims, " Who shall deliver me from this body of death?" Tennyson calls the body "this house, with all its hateful needs, no cleaner than the beast." May we not also cry, " Who shall deliver me from this heavily - handicapped idiosyncrasy of Being? What shall enable me to attain equilibrium?" What but the divinely-ordained counter-partal complement and supplement of our fatally finite one-sided Being? Spite of all the altruist may say, it is not merely the abstract realisation, but the subjective actualisation of the Ideal that we each of us require.

> " There is a world in each poor heart's domain
>   Of sense and action."

Of which it may logically be predicated—

> " If all mankind were safe in Heaven,
>   And I condemned to linger on a lonely earth,
>   I could not be content, in contemplation of the happy sky,
>   Dwelling with rapture on their gain, my dearth forgotten
>   In their blessedness.
>   Ah, no ! I too would share that perfect state."
>   —SOPHY SINGLETON.

The altruist, forgetting that Deontology is the synthesis of Egoity and Altruity, falls into the absurd by being " plus royaliste que le roi." Certainly Napoleon I. did not shrink from holocausts of sacrifice being offered up to him ; but surely the just man would recoil from this oriental expression of devotion from a fellow-creature, " I am your sacrifice ;" and " many a domestic tyrant would recoil from demanding wholesale the sacrifice of feeling, intelligence, and will which he or she extorts piecemeal from their ill-fated family." I say ill-fated, rather than unhappy, because it requires the capability of the conception of *l'idéal manqué* to *know* that you are unhappy.

Seeing that thought is a process consisting of the use of our faculties—of *feeling, intelligence,* and *will, each requiring to be equally represented for the evolution of a complete idea,* and *thus for the representation of the whole idea of Being to be possible*—it requires, by the terms, a whole, or complete Being to be present for ideal human nature to be fully represented, and for this the social unit alone is adequate.

A highly-developed brain may sustain a highly-complex consciousness, but it is only at the point of highest physiological activity that we find the psychological basis of a full consciousness. And this is never to be found in any finite individual; each one fails or is deficient somewhere. No one person's health of body and mind is absolutely sound or perfect.

Polarity represents perpetual motion or conflict with alternate victories between two forms of energy. The complementary pair lead not the life of the lotus-eater. The angel of Love, like the angel

Polarity or Duality.

that visited the pool of Bethesda, stirs up the waters of life, so that they may not stagnate. Thus is life made full of delightful surprises, which recreate instead of depressing the vitality and the faculties of each of the truly wedded pair. "Together, too, they fight the foe." The ancient Devil was man's hypostatised ideal of a thoroughly antagonistic Being. Hence we are disposed to call such persons a devil whenever we come across them. "Heat seeks an equilibrium by passing from hot to cold; no work can be got out of it in the reverse way;" heat being the positive, cold the negation of heat. Thus it is that one member of the conjugal pair must represent the positive, and the other the negative pole of Being with regard to each other; one must possess more spontaneous energy, and the other must be more receptive than impulsive. For spontaneous action to be realised, there must be, to a certain extent, a passive recipient of it; and for the negative character to be educed, it must be stirred up by a more positive one.

"Two of a trade never agree;" and two persons rather below par in spontaneous energy, thrust upon each other for life, would only cool to extinction of life. To boast of ourselves that we have no individuality or idiosyncrasy would be absurd upon the face of it. The bias towards the superactivity of one faculty which constitutes character is always at the expense of another; and thus the equilibrium of feeling, intelligence, and will, in which wholeness, holiness, or perfection of Being lies, is failed of being attained.

Thus the law of polarity is the key to the order of both the physical and spiritual universe. The positive argues the negative, and *vice versâ*; a negation argues a positively existent. As religion is the expression of the absolute by the relative, so is true conjugal love

H

the supreme expression of the attraction of spiritual equivalents of the perfect correlation of finite beings; each instinctively seeking perfection or completion through union with their opposite, as a chemical force rushes to its affinity. A thing, or object of thought, must be either more, or less than man, to be self-sufficient, self-poised, or self-existent. The principle of polarity is therefore the principle of duality, which must be recognised as the fundamental condition of the universe. Hence the "joy of life," through the sense of fulness, wholeness, or perfection of Being, is only actually experienced in *the union of true lovers.* What wonder, then, that their songs of praise fill such a large place in literature? Hence Plotinus says there are three who have the vision of the ideal —the poet, the saint, and the lover—their dream and their vision is alike of harmony. Poetry, and the arts, and sciences, bear witness to the fact of the adaptation of one thing to another, and so of the primordial design that instituted the universe.

"The improvement in the condition of women," says Samuel Laing, "has brought about a corresponding improvement in *the male sex, for the polarity between the two has come to be the most intimate and far-reaching influence of modern life.*" Polarity or contrast reaches its highest development in the highest civilisation, *i.e.,* the truest and the most spiritually cultured of the human race. Art is but the mimicry of the most supreme achievements of nature. As Emerson says, "The tender grace of an exquisitely sympathetic emotion becomes stereotyped into what is called good form in manners."

The mind of man does away with the hypothesis of accident, and the good for Being is the logically regarded end to which all things are working. "Knowledge dwells in heads replete with thoughts of other men" (Cowper). The knowledge of self is but a running accompaniment to all our other knowledge of man, God, and the universe. It is through and along with this knowledge, that all other knowledge is taken in. Self-consciousness is the thread on which the pearls of knowledge are strung. The *apprehension* of *relativity* is the fundamental necessity to which all finite intelligence is subject in the acquisition of knowledge. Moral purpose is *mind-purpose* or rational *purpose, i.e.,* purpose relating to Being, to wit, the German expression, "Ich hatt'es nicht übel gemeint," "I did not *mean* any harm." Evil-doing is a form of insanity of mind, indicating a partial action of some one particular faculty, as in hypnotism; a hypnotised person is not a moral agent.[1] Thought is a syllogism of which the conclusion is contained in the major premiss. "The term

Man'sOracle is within him. He reads his Destiny in the Abstract Ultimate Principles of Reason.

---

[1] "Order is ideal," says Lotze. "The purpose of the world is the production of happiness." Teleology is a part of order. "Teleology impresses an order on things not themselves produced *ad hoc*" (Lotze). "The Ideal is the heat that keeps all things fluid, and forms them anew at every moment." "Divine life may be represented *in ours* through an immanent Ideal."

mental activity, if retained, has to be construed as signifying not anything happening within the conscious content itself, but the full play of all that part of our extra-conscious psycho or extra-physiological Being, from which such sense-transcending conscious content is the supreme emanation" (E. Montgomery). The subject without an object cannot actualise itself, or its capacities; and even in reflection, it is on the impressions made upon us from without that we reflect, and ideally realise, referring them to the same categories of causality as in spontaneous representations. "Knowledge is the mirror of the world to us, but it is also a process by us" (Lotze).

Imagination has been defined as the capacity of evoking intuitive representations; yet the formation of generic images is distinct from abstraction.

Imagination. However, it can never free itself from the logic of facts except under the form of mere fancy, which is also built on modified representations of actual presentations. The postulates of reason are not mere assumptions or suppositions. This must be the meaning of Sir Isaac Newton's "Hypothesi non fingo." "To clear the mind of all prepossessions (or *à priori ideas*) would be to *clear the mind of itself.* All science is built on implicit trust in the fundamental prepossessions with which we are furnished, which, unless used vigorously, we cannot be said to have a *mind.*"

"Certainty lies in self-controlled thought," or

thought in strict accordance with reflective reason. With culture there accrues a reflective logical control over the psychical mechanism.

Certainty.

The ideal of education lies in the instilling of high intellectual, emotional, and moral standards of thought or mental representations, since it is by *feeling* that we arrive at a sense of Being, or a realisation of ourselves as a Sufficient Cause or *substans* of feeling ; by *intelligence* that we apprehend the relativity of our Being or the Efficient Cause of action; and by *the will*, or instinctive tendency of Being that we comprehend the Final Cause of action and Being. The world is only intelligised through being brought under the principle of self-consciousness. Lotze says, " Our joy is but an echo of that joy which sees its purpose realised in the goal of the universe." He adds, " It is in our *seasons of happiness* that we have *most Ideal* consciousness of God."

Ideal of
Education.

There must obviously be a preparatory education of all our faculties for the vital feelings of delight which characterise the union of true complementaries to take place ; for *not from the union of the spiritually undeveloped* **does true** *happiness spring.* Hence the first love of two adolescents or unevolved human beings has been properly called " calf-love." There may indeed exist a true physiological attraction between such a pair, but it is an awful thing for human spirits to be dragged down, and the whole of their future here clouded, by

Union of
True Com
plemen
taries.

absorption in their physical organism to the forgetting of their real or spiritual Being.   The physical
organism should only be the handmaid of the soul.
The yearning of true love is a spiritual longing
(*sehnsucht*) for the *spectre* of spiritual isolation and
imperfection of Being to be exorcised by union with
one nearer and dearer than all.   Count Tolstoi, in
" Anna Karénine," describes the pleasant spectacle of
a harvest-home amongst his peasantry.   Amid the
gambols of pleasure and shouts of triumph of his
rough tenantry, the master feels his own loneliness
accentuated the more.   " Who shall deliver me from
the feeling of the desert?" cries the lonely heart.
" Only real, or spiritual love, human and divine,
is the goal and the way."   This is the reply of
psychological science, including the witness of the
will and of the moral sense, for in it alone is true
harmony arrived at between the Creator, and His
rational creature, as also between all rational beings
throughout the universe.   Love is the harmony of
the internal Ego or subject with the external medium,
the non-Ego.   Lotze considered that the results of
science must be reconciled with human sentiment.
" Order without reference to the intrinsic worth of
the realities involved is inconceivable.   We have an
instinctive belief that harmony exists between the
mind of man and the universe " (Lotze).

Egoity, or the sense of individuality, furnishes self-
love.   Sympathy, or the sense of relativity, furnishes
social love, and the moral or practical sense which we call

the sense of duty, furnishes theopathy, or the adoration
of our Creator. Professor Drummond, in a charming
little work called " The Greatest Thing in
the World," says : " No other charge than
lovelessness need be preferred against any
one." Jesus said of the Magdalen, " Much
shall be forgiven her, because she hath
greatly loved." " Love is the rule for fulfilling all rules." " Not to love now, or in the present,
is to be an unloving person." Hence Count Tolstoi
says we must love each one for what they have of
goodness, spite of their shortcomings ; but he also
says that the particular relations in which each particular person stands to the world constitute him to
be what he is—*constitute* his particular individuality
—therefore to say that a heart can find *the joy* of the
complete *rest,* which results only from union with a
complementary being, in mere general benevolence,
is contrary to reason. Theodore Parker more truly
said that " Even the love of God cannot take the
place of the love of a fellow-creature, just as the love
of all our fellow-creatures cannot take the place of
the love of God." " Render therefore unto Cæsar
the things that are Cæsar's, and unto God the things
that are God's." That one thing is not another is
as true in the spiritual world as that two atoms
cannot hold one and the same place in space.[1]

Reason is Personal as well as Love. We attribute Value to that which exemplifies Ideal Life.

---

[1] Lotze, in stating his doctrine of Moral Idealism, says : " Value does
not reside in things excepting as they conspire to realise the *moral
Ideal, and this Ideal result is happiness.*" " Only the most nonsensical

Professor Drummond says, " Everything else in our lives is transitory but love." Love is the *summum bonum*, " because in the nature of things it is going to last—this is the reason why love should be the supreme thing striven after." Shadworth Hodgson has said, " Love is the one passion that has a future—hate expires with the extinction of its object." Professor Drummond says, " The final test of religion is love." " Even self-denial itself is nothing, is almost a mistake. Only a great purpose, or a mightier love, can justify the waste." " Nothing is a hardship to love." This is the yoke of which Jesus said, " My yoke is easy, and My burden light." " Through love alone do we come into contact with God or man." Count Tolstoi says, " Love is the only rational activity, is the only real life and real sign of life of the spirit of man," rational activity meaning activity relative to real, or noumenal Being. The rushing together of chemical forces is not immediately rational, although under the direction of a rational Being, such material conditions of psychological existence may be ultimately or mediately conducive to the good for Being. " The unity of matter and spirit is in their worth, not in their essence" (Lotze). Pure reason consists of the concepts arising necessarily in reflection on the Being of the subject-object, and on

mysticism believes in good that no one enjoys." " What is to be a good has the *only* and *necessary* locus of its existence *in the living feeling* of some spiritual (*i.e.*, Self-conscious) Being." " The Cosmic process is only the condition of producing a happy life.",

normal and typical Being, of which the Ideal is arrived
at by comparison. As *Justice,* according to Cicero,
involves the idea of proportion, so also does love.
Relations are hierarchical or graduated.

Love *par excellence,* or emphatically so-called, is
life set to the sweet melody or rhythm of dual Being.
Divine love is human life set to perfect
harmony with the Divine will. It has
been said of St. Augustine that, *not content*
to proclaim that which he had himself experienced,
" *he felt bound to incorporate that experience into*
a scheme of the universe to be transmitted to pos-
terity." Such is the feeling which has also prompted
this work. As Faraday knew that electricity is the
law of the physical world, so did St. Augustine
realise that Grace or Love is the law of the spiritual
creation : " c'est l'amour seul qui nous fait croire au
bien." The metaphysician deals with the real, the
enduring, as the laws of ontology are *found* in
spiritual *facts* and *formulated by man* through his
power of reflective reasoning. " Death
cannot touch the fadeless bloom of true or
spiritual Love, for we must for ever yearn
for our spiritual counterpart or complement. "Ouvrir
les bras, et las d'attendre, sur le néant les renfer-
mer, mais les bras toujours les lui tendre toujours
l'aimer" (Sully Prudhomme). The constructive form of
the law of polarity lies in metaphysics; in so building
up together the principles or attributes of Being that
one typical Personality stands out in its wholeness,

*Love
human and
Divine.*

*Spirituality
of True
Love.*

that thus it may better reflect the attributes of the Prototypal Being than can any separate idiosyncrasy.[1] Thus only do we arrive at a still faint, but fuller comprehension of the nature infinitely above us, as being absolute in power, wisdom, and goodness. One idiosyncrasy will best reflect *His power*, another *His wisdom*, and another *His goodness*. Only through the experience of our own spiritual Being, surviving the decay and destruction of its present shell (which tends to creeping or to sudden death), could we possibly have a clear insight into the essential nature of Being. Then will be separated the pearl from the shell, the grain from the husk. Consciousness, or cognition, is the condition of the consequent recognition of the ideal attributes of Being. Only through the dual affinity and union of two complemental spirits with the Divine nature can a really satisfying revelation of Deity be conveyed to the human spirit. "Those meet whose prayers meet," or tally one with the other. The more perfect our own being, the better will it mirror the Divine. One may be *content to wait* for an expected good, but *not logically content with the ultimate negation of the rationally, and therefore necessarily con-*

---

[1] "Knowledge is a process in which we, ourself, our mind, take an active part." "Noumenal Substance has the property, the idea (or necessary mental representation) of a Substance." "Self-consciousness is the characteristic of real personality; experience is naturally attributed to a person." "The elements of a Substance (as feeling, intelligence, and will) cannot be more real and primary than Substance itself."

ceived, *good or best for Being.* "Patience," says St. Gregory, "is noble *only when associated with love,*" and therefore with *hope.* "The best is always king," is an old saying. The French talk of going in for "*le petit bonheur*" and going by "*la petite vitesse*" with contempt. The more void of true joy our life here is, the less can our hearts conceive the joys belonging to a more advanced state of being, *i.e.,* of spiritual evolution. Christ said that the children of this world are wiser than the children of light, for they cleave to their ideal, whereas, through the weakness of the flesh, wiser men fall between the two ideals of spirituality and worldliness, or mistake other-worldliness for spirituality ; these are they who would make use of God, as they do of their fellow-creatures, for their own aggrandisement. But the idea of death, so beautiful to the twice born, has no charm for the worshippers of Mammon.

The action and reaction upon each other of complementary beings may be called systematic. As one *colour* is thrown up or enhanced by its requisite complementary—as red with green—and as these united in a spectroscope together present the full white ray, so it is with complementary spirits. By union they are merged as it were into one fuller or more perfect personality, one heart, one mind, one will, one quest of the Holy Grail of righteousness, one hope of the fulfilment of *the Ideal,* and so of eternal communion

Complementary Beings.

with the Father of Spirits.   Thus "*Love is not a vain thing for you, for it is your life,*" the true spiritual life, called into incessant action and reaction by the beloved.

> " Du mein Gedanke ! Du mein Sein und Werden,
>   Du meines Herzens erste Seligkeit,
>   Ich liebe dich, wie nichts auf dieser Erden,
>   Ich liebe dich in Zeit **und** Ewigkeit,
>   Ich denke dein—kann **stets** nur deiner denken,
>   **Nur** deinem Glück ist dieses Herz geweiht,
>   Wie dich auch mag des Lebens Schicksal lenken,
>   Ich liebe dich in Zeit und Ewigkeit,"
> " Du bist der Himmel mir bestimmt, mein anderes Selbst, *mein besseres Ich.*"

> "Thou art my soul, thou art my heart,
>   Nought can like thee such joy impart."

What wonder, then, that the history of humanity has been sad and unsatisfactory in spite of all its great discoveries in physics and metaphysics, made by one-sided, groove-ridden, individuals! The really important thing is not that a man, or woman, or the trappings of a horse should be adorned with pearls and diamonds ; or that we should travel with lightning speed from one end of the earth to the other ; or that the fall of infinitesimal bits of paper should sound to us like rattling of stones, as in a telephone ; or that our silly, mostly erroneous statements should be convey-able immediately we have ceased speaking, to other climes and future times.   No ; the really important thing is that our statements should be true and kind and pious ; that we should live a good

The **Real** **Important** Thing of Life.

life, hating all iniquity ; that we should love mercy,
and do justice, and walk humbly before God, blessing
and being blessed, and thus be prefitted even here
for entering into the still higher blessedness prepared from the beginning for all who love their Lord,
and do the will of the Father ; loving each other
more and more, and not the less, because of our
greater love of God. " I should have loved *thee less,*
loved I not virtue more." The *virtue of a thing is
truth to its nature.* The nature of a thing is determined by its relation to other things. It is through
the due fulfilment of our relations to other Beings,
and above all to the Supreme Being, that our individual evolution is accomplished ; hence some philosophers have insisted upon a man's deliberately
undertaking (*de propos fixe*) all domestic, civil, and
political functions, so that his whole nature may be
formally developed, but, as Mr. Grant Allen says
of "falling in love," "I believe things fall into a
truer order through natural attractions being acted
upon than by artificial determinations." The special
duty of each man lies in being *true* to the *peculiar*
faculties, with which he has been individually gifted.
Surely the same volitional determination will not be
expected of the man of two talents as of the man to
whom ten have been given. The silly phrase, " Il
y a un qui aime, et un qui se laisse aimer," has arisen
from the fact that for great nervous spontaneity of
action to be effective, and for reason to maintain its
control over passion, there must exist in one of the

two a cooler, more receptive temperament than in the other. Chacun donc aime à sa guise, selon son temperament ou sa manière d'être. Absolute analogues repel one another, as the positive and negative poles of two magnets only attract their opposites.

Nothing tends more to the *idée fixe* of insanity Idiosyncrasies than the unbalanced, uncompensated play Require to be Balanced. of our own idiosyncrasy.

Brahm, a German naturalist, says, "The male finds in the female those desirable attrac-Ideal Union. tive qualities which are wanting in himself.

> "Woman, 'tis thine to cleanse man's heart from every base unholy part,
> Thine in domestic solitude to teach him to be wise and good."

"Man seeks the opposite to himself with the *force of a chemical element.*"   "That which is true physically," says Laing, "is equally true of intellectual and moral (which includes emotional) characteristics." The harmony of the two depends on each of the two remaining more or less within the sphere of the polarity of his or her respective sex. A masculine woman and an effeminate man are equally unattractive, and the well-assorted union of the two in one gives a more complete harmony and reconciliation of opposites, than can be attained by the single individual. At present there are many men whose ideal might be summed up in the words of the Irish ballad :—

> "I'm fond of my pipe and the ladies
> And I'd make a most illigant Turk."

And George Eliot speaks of women who walk in rapture, with the consciousness of being dressed in the height of the fashion.

Evidently, under the influence of such ideals, the weaker party does not get fair play, and laws which are the result of centuries of male legislation show ignorance of the truth of the homely maxim, "That which is sauce for the goose is also sauce for the gander." For ideal union there must be identity or equality of essence, developing itself in opposite directions, the one supplementing what is wanting in the other. It has been said of love, "E'en the lost obey thee, weeping evermore," and certainly people would not *play* or *do* "being in love" so sedulously if they did not think it "*the thing*," or what spiritualists call *the Ideal.*

"The stability of the union of two substances depends partly *on the stable structure of its component elements, partly on the mutual affi-* Stability of nity being strong enough to keep them Union—on what it depends. together in presence of the attractions of other outside elements." The tendency of all substances is to fall back from a less stable to a more stable condition, and such a falling back is always attended with an evolution of heat; whilst, on the other hand, heat disappears whenever the elements of a more stable substance are made to enter into a less stable condition. "In chemical affinity a molecule drops one of its factors and takes on another, to which its attractions are stronger. Thus, when iron rusts in water, it is because the oxygen atom drops hydrogen to take iron. The displaced atom finds a refuge in one more congenial to it." "The tendency of all change is towards stability." It is the same with unstable human affinities or attractions. All are but *essays in true love*, that being the one stable, because essentially required, and so unfading, emotion.

> "Nothing is steadfast, nothing is true,
>   But your love for me, and my love for you,
>   My dearest, dearest heart."
>
> —*Song by Sullivan.*

Others come and go: children grow up, and change, only the *essentially* united remain together. For this, says the Scripture, shall a man leave his father and his mother and all his kindred. Still, although the united complementaries may together, as they cannot apart, reflect the pure white ray of absolute or perfect Being, yet that ray will be faint and dim in proportion to the lack of power, wisdom, and goodness of the individuals together representing it. Thus pure metaphysics must always exist as abstract ideas. This, however, it shares with mathematics, which are not, however, considered invalid on that account.

Æsthetics and the art of government have also their abstract ideals or laws, to which the

Abstract generalisations.

artist and the politician ought to conform, to be a true artist and a really wise ruler, although the word *ought* has been pronounced a fig- ment of fancy by a gifted physiologist of to-day.

The *proper function of reflection is to furnish us with ideals of the true, the beautiful, or harmonious, and the good or the felt* "ought to be." In reflection the single verified perception is generalised with regard to Being, or existence in the abstract. The single apprehension of a relation between persons or things is conceived as a general law of relation, and the comprehension of the real goodness and kindness of one act becomes a predicate or categorical imperative of duty, seeing that it is conducive to the truest welfare of Being. The one great want of mankind *is a common standard of truth, beauty, and goodness,* from which there could be no more appeal, than there is from the rules of arithmetic. Men must cease to separate the *ideals of truth, and love, and goodness* from *the ideal of happiness, for they are one and indivisible.* As real happiness lies in the fulfilment of these Ideals, so there is nothing to be proud of in feeling satisfied, simply through not having any Ideal to fulfil.

Liberty is the condition of the moral *will :* hence the strenuous efforts after it by heroes of all times. As wrong lies in the reflective or self-conscious choice of evil or the bad for Being, so good lies in the righteous choice of the good or best for real or spiritual Being. Ignorance is *un*-morality, like that of the lower animals. *Immorality* is the conscious breaking of the moral law. *Motive is the seal of morality ;* the external act *signifies nothing but the motive which prompted it.*

Right and Wrong. Evil is the Shadow of Liberty.

I

Bentham says the words *right* and *wrong* have no other meaning than that such or such actions ought, or ought not to be done. By the word *ought* is understood that every action should be in accordance with the *duty owed to our Creator*, to whom we are responsible for right action, or action according to His moral law. Thus we pray in our churches, "Lord, incline our hearts to keep this law." The primary laws of humanity were negative—"Thou shalt do *no* murder; thou shalt *not* steal." The *morality of culture* or *evolution is more advanced, i.e., positive*—"Thou *shalt love thy neighbour as thyself*, and the *Lord thy God with all thy might.*"

The identification of philosophy with religion is what the intellectual require, as the identification of

Identification of Philosophy with Religion.

religion with philosophy is the desideratum of the emotional and moral. The appeal to consciousness is the basis of the religious sentiment — sentiment meaning the combination of feeling, thought, and judgment. Sir William Hamilton says :—"Consciousness is to the philosopher what the Bible is to the Christian." The French expression, "la conscience de soi," represents both consciousness and what we emphatically call *conscience*. The principle of finality is the principle of morality. The good for Being, its eternal welfare, is what it points to. "Introspective self-consciousness, sense of personality, is the culminating form of mind. Mind thus acting as a whole has a superior form of activity to spontaneous mentality," which is partial, as in a person hypnotised artificially, or through an *idée fixe,* which is incipient insanity. Henri Greville's story of "Louwitch" is a remarkable instance of the latter.

Pure philosophy *has for its aim the grasping of the whole content of reason.* The mystery of religion is solved in the light of the principles of reason : the principles of causality, from which the mind, *tacked* as it is upon them, cannot free itself.[1] *Superstition does but mistake causes,* not deny causality. Metaphysic or ontological science, treats of the sense-transcending ideas of the philosophy of spirit. The word *ought* in its practical sense means *instant obedience to reason or conscience,* the *voice of God within us :* the oracle which has but one utterance: "Do the right thing," *i.e.,* that which is ruled by reason and conscience, "now and always." Utilitarianism regards consequences instead of the *à priori* fundamental principles of Reason. In saying, as is the fashion of the present day, *that there is no science of Being,* the principle of contradiction is violated, for the dictates of conscious experience are contradicted. The courts of law, *particularly of criminal law,* render this profession of *un*-faith ridiculous ; for

---

[1] "Man's real, inner, eternal life, which lies deeper down even than thought itself, the immediate activity of which is conditioned by the neural mechanism, is an infinite thing compared with the indications of it ; conduct is but a partial exhibition of Being. In all the higher range of feeling we know how soon the limit of expression is reached and that there are worlds of love, of pity, of sympathy, and *self-consecration* beyond what lips or even countenance can render, whilst sometimes feelings, and intuitions surge up from these hidden depths, spite of the conscious self-determination of the individual."

thereto we see persons summoned, first, on the ground of their personal existence ; and secondly, on that of their breach of the moral law, or Principle of Final Cause which, according to Leibnitz, is the law by which spiritual monads move, whereas physical monads are moved from without by the law of Efficient Causation.[1]

Horace says, "True happiness is to no spot confined, so you preserve a calm and equal mind."   But **True Happiness.** if I have written to any purpose, it is to show that the perfect equilibrium of the faculties is never seen in any single finite being, but only in the social unit, or the union of two perfectly complementary or well-matched individuals.   In saying with Spenser, "It is the mind that maketh good or ill," we mean that conformity with the reflective Ideals of Reason constitutes the test of truth, of beauty or harmony, and of goodness.   We recognise the same idea in Shakespeare's well-known words :—

> " Nothing is good, or evil, but thinking makes it so."

If a person can say "I *meant* well," it will be "accounted to him for righteousness," even though the effects produced by the act might have been mistaken.   *Thus are we satisfied in approaching to likeness to the Prototypal Being,* the Creator, "in whom is no darkness at all," who knoweth no change, because He was, and is, and always must be per-

---

[1] The doctrine most peculiar to Leibnitz is "the Individuality of everything *real,* and the Harmony of all things," only what partakes of the Essence of the Deity did he hold to be eternal. He maintained that there cannot be an ultimate explanation without an *Immaterial Principle,* which to explain—*the Harmony of everything*—must be *one and universal.* "Real ty means Individuality."

fection's self. Reflection is of the spirit within. We leave what is of the earth earthy out of account when we are reckoning with our real selves as to how we have kept the moral law. Reflection is the seal of reasoned conclusion as to our own Being and to that of our Creator, and as to the existence of the external Cosmos.

As utter insensibility is the proof to us of death, or death in life, so radiant happiness or intense realisation of life at its fundamental springs of feeling, intelligence, and will, presents the exhibition of life and Being at its apogee. In this world Happiness; of grief, wild discontent, destitution, and Love the Fulfilling of the Law. ofttimes madness, one would be tempted to assert that Goodness is wanting, did not the still, small voice of *conscience, as reason,* bear witness within us that we needs must learn through trials and difficulties of every description both to *know* and to *love* the law of Wisdom, and to bear her mild yoke before we can be capable of feeling happiness, for only then can we even understand what it means. Surely for a person to have a right to pronounce themselves happy, they ought to know what happiness means. A great love brings us more than anything to the feet of the Lord and Giver of the love which is true joy, that alone leading us to the feeling of universal benevolence. Contrasts or opposite polarities are necessary complements of each other's existence. How can we love the stranger we have not seen if we love not the brother we have seen? Only through our counterpart, do we learn sympathy with natures diametrically opposite to our own. Hence, love in itself has been said to be "the fulfilling of the law." " Her sins, which are many, are forgiven," said Jesus, "for she loved much." Again, how shall he who hath not loved the brother he has seen, love the invisible Father? And how shall he who hath never loved "*nearly and dearly*" feel *tenderness* and show *considerateness* for the far apart and uncongenial? Whereas, when a man truly loves one woman, all women are sacred to him because of their sisterhood with *her;* although, strange to state, a famous Professor of the present day has enunciated in one of his works that " it would be as rational to say that the nigger is the equal of the Caucasian as to say that woman is equal to man." And, equally, when a woman is truly and devotedly attached to one man, she feels a certain respect for all men, either for what they *are, or what they may become when purged from earthly grossness.* Bayard Taylor spoke of the eternal joy that man is to woman, and woman to man. Even Goethe wrote of "die ewige Weibliche," "l'éternel feminin," as a part of the order of the universe.

This, then, is the new theory of Idealism that I venture to offer to the reflecting public. It is perhaps well that all new theories are met with mistrust. The Chinese are so conservative that under one of their emperors, it *was death to compose a new tune;* but few are the theories that admit of *so direct* an application to one's own internal or rational experience as this one of the *necessarily dual construction of the Ideal of Being*, in which the opposite of each idio-syncrasy is represented, so that together the two may in reflective reasoning furnish a complete ontological ideal—an actual representation of its required attributes, *i.e.*, of the *three modes of causality* which underlie the constitution of the universe in the Divine essence. Can we suppose the histories of individuals and of the race to be and have been, like an idiot's story, all sound and fury, *signifying* nothing beyond this imperfect state of Being? Is the end of the rat and the toad, and of the sage, the poet, and the saint, conceivably the same? "Car c'est de nos conceptions rationelles qu'il s'agit." Then, as Tennyson says, the howlings and ragings of the monsters of the primeval slime were as mellow music matched with this hideous discordance of *means with end.* "Much ado about nothing" might then be written on the tombstones of the wisest and best, who, as St. Paul says, would in that case be of all men the most miserable, the sensual having revelled in their sensuality, the wicked in carrying out their evil will; only Idealists such as Plato and Socrates, together with the saints of all the Churches, will not have realised their Being, their faith, their love, their hope. I will not offend altruists, whose hearts are above (*sic*) the desire of happiness, by a direct allusion to so *low* a desideratum, for the very good reason that Love is Heaven, and Heaven is Love, so that love cannot be con-

sidered apart from joy. Thus St. Paul could rationally say, " Rejoice always."

> " Wer seine Wille hat,
>   Hat die ganze Welt."

*In the instinctive tendency to seek his own welfare
and to sympathise with that of his fellows*, man is
furnished with the rational intuition that the well-
being or beatitude of humanity, as such, is the will of
his Creator, or His purpose in His creation—the beginning of a work always standing in logical relation to
its end. We find it written in Genesis, " Man shall
be as a god, knowing good from evil, and choosing
between them." Now, apart from relations to Being,
what conception of good can we frame ? It is, however, true that, in different stages of egoistic actualisation, our idea of the *good* greatly varies. As it
is in *the exercise of its faculties that a creature
finds enjoyment*, it is scarcely to be wondered at
that the Stoics put the chief joy of man in exercis-
ing his *master-faculty—that of reason and rational
choice in action*. But as reason requires *feeling*
or passion upon which to *exercise itself*, the kindly
Epicurus was nearer the mark when anticipating
Goethe in proclaiming that " Feeling is everything."
Christ taught the same when He summed up the
whole duty of man in the words, "*Love thy neighbour as thyself, and the Lord thy God with all
thy powers.*" Faith and hope are but the beautiful
followers or outcome of love ; *therefore, whilst love*

remains, we cannot despair; and if we require a **reason** for the faith, love, and hope that is a part of our human constitution, **the only** sufficient and most satisfactory reason **for their** existence **is** that they are the necessary products, **fruits, or conse-**quences of *our intelligence, our heart, and our will*—what St. Paul calls " **fruits of the spirit,**" *i.e.,* fruits of spiritual evolution.

The Hebrew Scripture says, "Mark the perfect man, and behold the upright; *the end of that man shall be peace.*" This is the prophecy or protesting forecast of reason against the apparent moral topsy-turvy of this world. *Peace* always implies *hope* through faith in the necessary postulates of reason. Cherbuliez says, "Le ridicule ne peut **pas durer**" (*ci vuol pazienza*), the ridiculous being *self-contradiction,* **which is the** logical **test or** *reductio ad absurdum,* applied **in this case to the idea of the end of** the **dog and the man being the same.** "**How** few realise that there can be no higher **test of truth for** any man than that *he is himself!*" "Je pense, donc *je suis,*" said Descartes. **The day** on which a man does **not move out of the way of a** railway train or **of a** conflagration, we may believe him when he says he does not believe in the existence **of** matter, or in **that of his own** physical organism. **The day** on which he ceases to provide helpful and pleasant **things for** himself and his children, to send for the doctor when he, or they **are** sick or ailing, we **may believe that he does not desire to be** happy or

The End in view.

enjoy life ; and on the day that he ceases to endeavour after a political constitution, which may pro-
tect his rights as a man, we may believe that he is
sincere in being *a pessimist* of the school of Schopenhauer; whereas the rational optimist bears trials, as St.
Paul says, joyfully, certain that the object of them
is that he may become fitter for the free exercise of
his will and the enjoyment that comes therefrom in
a better and happier state of Being.   The endeavour
to realise the Ideal of Being, is the real Quest of
the Holy Grail.   " Be ye perfect, as your Father in
Heaven is perfect," is *le dernier mot de la morale.*

The following lines sound like an echo of one of
Robert Browning's last poems :—

> "O figure voilée et vague en mes pensées,
>   Rencontre de demain que je ne connais pas.
>   O paraît si tu peux encore électriser
>   Ce miserable cœur, *sans désir* et sans flamme ;
>   Me rendre *l'infini dans un regard de femme,*
>   *Et toute la nature en fleur dans un baiser.*
>   Viens ! comme les marins d'un navire en détresse
>   Jettent pour vivre une heure un trésor à la mer.
>   Viens ! je te promets tout, âme et cœur, sang et chair,
>   Tout pour *un seul instant de croyance ou d'ivresse.*"
>   —FRANÇOIS COPPÉE.

It is a truism to say that without faith, love, and
hope, nothing but despair remains.   " The just shall
live by faith."

" Alienation from reason comes to much the same
as alienation of reason," just as " none are so deaf as
those who will not hear."   To draw inferences of
reason from the nature of every other thing except-

ing *from the nature of our own Being*, is such an
unfair, and above all *irrational*, proceeding, that it is
not worth while commenting on. As without sun
and rain and air the flower withers, so the human
soul without *faith, without love, without hope* (that is
to say, shorn of the ontological outcome of reason),
falls far below the lower animals in wretchedness, and
is very apt to revert to their sensuality, to make up
for the loss of spiritual vitality—*corruptio optima
pessima* (the corruption of the best is the worst).
Droz says, " La société d'aujourdhui *n'est dupe de rien
que d'elle même.*" As little children in their play
say, "Let us pretend to be ladies and gentlemen," so
the children of a larger growth now seem to say,
"Although we act always *as if there were a moral
sense, and a Being to whom we are responsible for obedience to reason*, which is the law He has imposed, one
may say, *even on Himself*, let us *pretend to believe that
we have no sense of duty, and no intuition of a Being
to whom duty is owed; and although we are ourselves
presentations of the law of causality in its three modes,
let us make-believe that causality only means casual
succession of events in time* and space, burying our
heads in the sand, like the ostrich, *so as to conceal from
ourselves the fact* that our *perceptions, apprehensions,*
and *comprehensions* are *all based upon the* triform
causality which *constitutes the principle of Sufficient
Reason.*" " La façon dont un homme juge est une
indice certaine sur la façon dont lui-même doit être
jugé." " Excellence receives no hurt from the slights

of the world, as the sun is unimpaired by the darkness of our night" (Arabian). "La Providence nous
a donné juste assez de raison pour nous guider vers
elle." The adaptation of means to ends implies intelligent purpose or spiritual Personality. "If God were
mixed up with matter, He could not control it ; at least
such is the inference of reason from our own experience
in sickness of body and insanity of mind, *i.e.*, disorder
of the nervous system. Seeing that the *idea of a
Supreme Being*, perfect in power, wisdom, and goodness (the attributes of Ideal Personality), is *entirely
the outcome of reflective reason*, it is truly curious to
hear it condemned as *irrational*, or the contradiction
of reason to maintain it. Design proper being for the
good for Being, Being must precede rational design ;
design signifying the adaptation of means to an end.
All desires relate to Being ; so does *all purpose; so
does all understanding of similarity and difference.*
" Chemical analysis shows that our food is composed
of the same chemical elements that go to make up our
body." Here we see the attraction of *like for like
taught by Empedocles*, whilst the *Atomists* taught
that the combinations and separations of *atoms* were
similarly determined. " On n'est pénétrant qu'à la condition d'être facilement pénétrable. C'est la sensibilité
qui raffine le jugement. C'est sur son *propre cœur*
qu'on aiguise la lame dont on fouille l'âme d'autrui."

" That *which we are, we are.* One equal temper of heroic hearts,
  Made weak by time and fate, but strong in will
  To strive, to seek, *to find and not to yield.*"—TENNYSON.

The arts of the drama, music, and dancing testify to our need of joy, and other deep emotions.

The Greek fable of Pandora losing all the goods of life excepting *hope*, *is a simple truth of human experience;* but of course this hope *cannot refer to the invalid's prospects in this life*, but to hope *in our Creator* for *a future beyond the grave*, where the *justice and mercy of the Supreme Being will be justified* in the ultimate *happiness of all His rational creatures.* "I come to draw all men unto me," said Jesus. "He who dwelleth in love dwelleth in God," who is perfect Benevolence, or Love. Hence we say "God is Love," as God is Truth or the Reality: the real Being, from whom we spring: the Cause of Causes. Anaxagoras was the first who announced that *Reason was the cause of all the order in the world.* Aristotle compliments Anaxagoras because he was the first to introduce into philosophy the conception of *end or Final Cause.* To Leibnitz we are indebted for formalising the Principle of Sufficient Reason.

Surely, then, the addition inpsychology of rational consciousness, and of reflective *self*-consciousness and judgment therefrom, to physical or *unconscious attraction*, cannot be supposed to diminish the force of this constructing principle of both the physical and psychical universe. So far from this being the case, it is only when reflective reason has idealised, and so *spiritually realised*, the psychological experiences of the individual, that he, or she, fully comprehends them, giving them their allotted place under the fundamental laws, or order of the universe, and thus redeeming them from a selfish individualism. Thus, in the moral axiom, "Do unto others as you would be done by," our own rights are as patent as are our duties to others. This is how it is that man alone, of all the animal creation (to which he is *physiologically* allied), "sees before and after," through his reflective or speculative reason, tracing back the same order that now prevails in the past, and forecasting the reign of the same order in the future, according to the law of the non-contradiction of experience. *Intellect*, or *Self*-evidence, *as the representation of Being*, and so of Sufficient Cause and Sufficient Reason, *is the universal of thought.*

The sequences of cause and effect are Nature's promises, and if she does not keep them, and we do not observe them, life will break down. "Faith in cause and effect is the foundation of all stable life, and all regular progress (or evolution) in the individual and in the race." "The savage has not faith enough to see the harvest in the seed." Through reflective reason we learn to put more and more confidence in the *laws of causality*, Sufficient, Efficient, and Final, so that we use alike these three laws mechanically, as we do numerals, not immediately realising their essential import at every moment. The sense of Sufficient Cause is that of the intelligent form of the energy put forth, which is the characteristic of noumenal or spiritual Being. "Our cate-

Cause and Effect.

gories of thought are in harmony with the universe, though they are *ideal*. Belief is based on the harmony of the external world with the internal Being of man. *Only such beliefs do we call rational.*" Hence we logically predicate that what is true of a *thing*, is true of its *kind* or like. *Representation is in the ratio of presentation.* Thus we judge action to be *right*, or the *thing ruled*, when it accords with the principle of Sufficient Reason, and wrong when it is opposed to that law of our reflective nature which is the seat of conscience or the sense of responsibility to our Creator to keep His law. Joy is the positive, sorrow the negative of feeling. We feel sorrow at the *coming short* of the ideal in ourselves and others. *Blasphemy is the negation of it in the Supreme Being.* Sadness and ennui are the attendants of the absence of self-actualisation, or of Ideal realisation of Being. Only to man is given the Ideal life of pure reason, *i.e.*, of transcendental or *sense*-transcendent representations of pure or real Being : yet unevolved man, or man not "born again to the spirit" of reflective reason, which is that of righteousness or piety, leads a life but little removed from that of the lower animals, his motto being "Let us eat, drink, marry, and be merry, for to-morrow we die." Perhaps it may be asked here, Wherefore is a being destined to a higher life and to communion with the Supreme Being, connected so closely by his physical organisation with the lower animals? The answer to this is obvious. How could we have understood, and so been able to control, the animal creation to our uses, if we had stood in no relation to them? But this is no reason for our forswearing our higher birth of kinship with the Father of Spirits, our Creator and our Judge.

It is our reflective ideals that prevent our conduct being determined at random by external impressions.

Invisible realities.   "A man should have the consent of his whole nature for what *he does and what he is.*" "There is a want of hearty vision that invisibles are realities." "God is on the side of those who are on His side." Love is the real philosopher's stone, turning everything into gold. The *spontaneous recognition of similars or their reflective logical substitution being the condition of objective knowledge, the transcendental subject and the transcendental object are of one kind.* "*That which corresponds to our ideas is the object.*" It is *apperception or reflective self-consciousness which is the constitutor of the unity of perception, apprehension,* and *comprehension.* For the prospect of the hereafter to have any hold upon the heart, there must be *expectation of the renewal of the intensest spiritual joys we have experienced here.* The *scientific axiom* of·the persistence or continuity of force involves, as a necessary corollary, the persistence of the relations between forces. "Now the idea of *force* is the reflective outcome of Being, of which energy is the expression, just as the idea of the relations and correlations of forces is the *outcome of ontological or spiritual relations and correlations.*"

" C'est *parcequ'on se cherche, qu'on s'aime,* parce-qu'il y a problème incessant que l'on est attiré l'un vers l'autre." Il y a dans l'homme la nos-talgie du bonheur, la nostalgie de l'infini, the *Ahnung* (craving for) of a possible completion of his own being by that of a helpmeet unto him. "Chacun voit un autre, et le juge selon ses propres gouts et ses propres besoins. *Comment pourrait on le considérer en dehors des impressions qu'il nous cause*—en dehors des liens (relations) qui nous unissent à lui ?" " La posses-sion n'est pas de ce monde ; nos lèvres n'ont pas eu encore le temps de dire, 'J'aime,' que ce mot est déjà transformé en un melancolique, ' *J'aimais,*' et *en un joyeux ' J'aimerai.*'" " *La tendresse est le rêve d'un rapprochement poussé jusqu'a l'absorption. Plus près, toujours plus près ; voila l'idéal de l'amour ;* l'attraction physique n'est que *l'image* de l'attraction de l'âme." "Le besoin per-petuel d'assimilation se trouve dans le monde moral comme dans le monde physique." "Only those who love can be sure of love," as only the malevolent know the full meaning of hate. " Le verbe *constate nos sentiments* (stamps them with the added impres-sion of reflective reason) *et ainsi les intensifient.*" *The association of the ideas of reason arise out of the harmony of the elements or properties of Being.* " The idea of *end* or Final Cause is borrowed from consciousness."

Leibnitz's distinction between physical and spiri-

Sehnsucht: the Instinct of the Duality of Being

tual monads is the most exhaustive. He says,
"Physical monads *are moved* by Efficient

Final Cause, Perfection of Being.

Causes (these being external relations) as
the connection of the lower animal with its
physical organism; whereas spiritual monads *move*
from within." Reflective man acts from his own
ideals of the true, the harmonious or beautiful, and
the good—his freedom of will lying in his power to
choose what seems to him best, or the best for the
preservation of the integrity of his spiritual Being.
"Being is the explanation of everything." As the
sense of finality involves the evolution of Being, so
the sense of relativity in its most harmonious form
suggests Efficient Causation. *Love*, emphatically so
called, *is the choice of the felt fittest to one's own
Being, not of what will be most admired by other
people.*

The unprogressiveness of the nations who practise
polygamy, as the Chinese and the Turks, demon-

Order of Nature and Reason.

strates its fundamental opposition to reason
and to the evolution of personality. Happiness cannot be supposed to accompany
defiance of the order of Nature and reason. *If all
order be only rationally conceived as for the good
for Being, nothing but obedience to it can consciously produce our well-being. From our sense
of freedom of choice, the existence of the reflective sense of sin and of repentance is therefore
explained.* Mons. Renouvier says, "Rights and
duties *are deductions* (reflective) *from the concept*

of the good, not ultimate conceptions. Evolution is not contradictory of creation." Memory is the faculty by which the traces of past *really felt* or *truly received impressions are preserved.*" "Notre vie passée s'y réfléte comme dans un miroir." "*Our idea of the uniformity of Nature comes from the uniformities of our experience*" (Maudsley). We cannot, *properly* speaking, logically or *really conceive* the *contradiction of experience*, seeing that our conceptions are of experiences generalised *through the elimination of all accidental circumstances.* A friend once said to me, "How do you derive the conception of a happy life for man hereafter from our unhappiness here?" Now, the answer I offer to this question is, that as when the chrysalis bursts into the butterfly with wings outspread, we conclude that from being a creeping thing, he has passed into a creature of the air and light; so also, when man is born again to the spirit of reflective, or sense-transcending reason, he sees in his faculties of faith, love, and hope in goodness, the forecast or prophecy of a future life "beyond the cloud and beyond the tomb;" otherwise these faculties would be wreckers' lights or will-o'-the-wisps, which is inconceivable of a rationally-constituted universe; but, as Shelley says, "the height of these faculties transcends our physical organs." "O Lord," prayed an American preacher over a deathbed, "take him to *heaven to his friend, or any way, take him where his friend is,*" evidently judging that if his love were extinguished his faith and hope would be so also. " Thou Soul of the Universe, that art the eternity of thought." "*Evolution and Teleology are correlative terms— an observed order always being for an end or purpose.*"

"*Men can interpret others only by the terms of their own nature.*" We each of us prefer a certain kind of bodily nutriment because *it agrees with us*, because we can "*assimilate or as-self it.*" As the stomach repels that which it cannot digest, so our mind revolts at ideas of truth, beauty, and goodness which are the contradiction of its own. They produce in us a sense of unreality, a sort of suicidal scepticism as to the existence of reality, harmony, benevolence. Joy, or happiness, is positive, arising out of the spontaneous actualisation or out of the reflective realisation of our ideals; whereas distress and grief are negative, arising out of "a pining for what *is not*" according to ideal expectation. The happy lover is a case of the former, the poet and sage of the latter. Although memory is as moon-light unto the sunlight of happy experiences, *still it is a positive ground of hope.* What has happened to *the spirit may also happen to it again,* although all that *is of the body perishes with the body.* When Christ left His disciples for another sphere He said, "My Spirit I leave with you,"—the spirit of reflective reason, upon whose inductions and deductions, the science of Being, and its destiny, like all other sciences, is based; the nature of a thing giving the clue to its destiny, or destination, the conscious process of deliberate reasoning making *explicit* what *was implicit*.

> "Denn mit **dem** Weltgeist selbst zu ringen,
> Wird unserer Kräfte Hochberuf."—GOETHE.

"They who seek to *transcend the conditions under which alone knowledge is possible* are," in Goethe's words, "as wise as little children, who, when they have looked into a mirror, turn it around to see what is behind it." Not Being itself, but consciousness is the object of knowledge. **As we** believe the evidence of our senses with regard to physical objects of mental representation, so do we intuitively trust the report of our inner senses of emotion, intellection, and volition, with regard to our rational representations of spiritual objects. Actions are prompted by desire, or tendency, and guided by the intelligence, or intuition of causality. As the past must have contained the germs of the present, so the present must contain the germs of the future. "It is through the *Holy Spirit of reason* that man enters into communion with God ; the unintelligible awakens *no real spiritual emotion in us.*" Even men's stubborn resistance to a new doctrine, testifies to their instinctive expectation of understanding things. "It is a very touching sight to see one human soul asking forgiveness of another *for the breach of a law tacitly understood to be binding alike* upon both — the *unwritten* law worked by God into the constitution

(margin note: Of the Conditions of finite Being, and finite Knowledge.*)*

of our mind, heart, and conscience." The criminal code of every civilised people is based on this un-written law—or rather, of this law that is "graven on the fleshy tablets of the heart," heard by the ear of reason alone—thus *there is a tacit understanding between all civilised nations,* that he who breaks the moral law in the form of committing murder or theft, of bearing false witness, or of removing his neigh-bour's landmark, or of cruelty and injustice in all its myriad forms, is not only responsible to God, but also to his fellow-men, from whose society he becomes an outcast when he thus forfeits the right to its protec-tion. "To assimilate a thing is to as-self it." "*In-dividuality is the condition and exponent of unity of conception.*" Who then can object to Individuality ? terming it selfishness, with which word Egoity has been so funnily confounded, seeing that both Altruity and Deontology depend upon Egoity, the source of all conception. "Disagreement with us is always *disagreeable,* because of the difficulty or the impos-sibility of *our assimilation of it into our own system of conception.*" *To each and every one a thing is neither more nor less than "what he thinks it"* (Maudsley). Only through their relations to our self are the properties of a thing *knowable by us.* To say a thing is cold, means that it makes us feel cold ; to say a thing is hard, means that it resists our pres-sure. Oman Khayyam says :

> " Heaven's but the vision of fulfilled desire,
>   And Hell the shadow from a soul on fire."

" The thought-kindling accident is imitated by scientific experiments."

"An eternal thinking subject is the correlation of Nature." Kant identifies freedom with determination of reason. "To say Nature is uniform is an *True freedom.* identical proposition," Nature meaning for us the cosmos' unchanging universal order. "*The idea has no reality except as a part of consciousness.*" Happiness and duty are not opposed, neither are belief and evidence. Although "there is a divinity that shapes our ends, rough-hew them how we will," necessity is not absolutely opposed to liberty, seeing that even a tethered animal has a certain amount of liberty of action ; nor is evolution the contradiction of creation, although they are called antinomies. " The *ordo ad individuum* and the *ordo ad universum* are built out of a common stock," *i.e.*, the self-consciousness of noumenal Being. The human cerebro-neural mechanism answers the same purpose for us *in its automatic action as do external machines of our own construction,* sparing us manual labour ; whereas in the latter case it is mental effort that is spared us. Still our reason must always be awake to prevent our becoming the slaves of *custom* and of *words,* that most insidious of slavery. The unrest of dissatisfaction is the instrument which *Nature uses to prevent our stagnating in feeling, intelligence, and will.* "It is in making the initial start *that a mind emancipated has its chief uses.*"

If the dialectic process of the association of the

fundamental ideas of reason in reflection were

thoroughly understood, accepted, and acted upon, the dominion of Faith, Love, and Hope would be daily more extended throughout the human race, and expediency would make way for action according to the morality of principle. Homes would indeed be anticipations of heaven, and emotional, intellectual, and moral progress would advance in geometrical instead of arithmetical ratio. It is through *reflective reason that we realise* that the principles implicit in the individual mind are made explicit for all thinkers, *they commanding both the moral and the monetary capital which enable us to carry out our greatest and noblest purposes.* " Reflective introspection is the highest mental activity, in the abeyance of which the elements of normal Personality are prone to fall asunder, working themselves out with an automatic regularity, and relative independence," as in hypnotic states. The antithesis to this is that moral force (reflective reason) in the healthy individual, whereby the sacred unity of Personality is realised. But automatism is nevertheless visible in the phenomena of distraction, instinct, habit, passion. But these should be in subjection to the realisation of Personality, from which proceed self-reverence, social regard (or sense of relativity and correlativity), and reverence for the authority of the Divine Author of our own and all Being, out of which the sense of duty springs ; these answering to the principles of

Sufficient, Efficient, and Final Causality. As feeling is the test of fact, so reflective reason is the guarantee of truth. It is through it that we know that we feel, and *what* we feel, and that we know *what* we intelligise, or what we know, and that we determine ourselves morally for the Supreme Good, or *summum bonum.* Pagan philosophy and Christianity are unanimous about the importance of the latter point. Seneca said, "Nothing can really hurt a man, but what hurts or deteriorates his soul;" and Christ said, "What shall ·it profit a man, if he gain the whole world, and lose his own soul?"

The passage from superstition to religion is simply the substitution of conceptual Idealism for imaginative Idealism or Myth; for even superstition acknowledges and postulates causality, whilst strangely enough ignoring the relation of identity between cause and effect, and hence assuming altogether irrelevant causes for given effects, and adopting means that are contradictory of the end or final cause of Being. What Christ especially taught was that human love is the means to the end of divine love, ascetics of all times and places having regarded its suppression as most important to virtue, and they have, moreover, required the exclusion of our own happiness as the means to the end of the happiness of others, but only when they make some one else eat their own dinner, take their rest in sleep, and take possession of their own wife and children, shall we be able logically to believe this profession of unnatural, and so of unreal holiness; for the voice of reason, which is the voice of God within us, proclaims, "I will have obedience, not sacrifice," saith the Lord. Even when faith has passed into sight, and hope into fruition, love remaineth, and must remain for ever. The data for all argument concerning our Creator are only to be found in reflective apperception of our own Being.

Matthew Arnold, in a beautiful poem entitled *The Hidden Life*, says: "Sometimes at the touch of a beloved hand, we seem to know whence our life came and where it flows." Here we have human love revealing to us the loving Father. In a famous Hindoo poem, Arjoun (Adam) entreats the Supreme Being to reveal Himself to him in the fulness of His power and His wisdom, but sinks fainting beneath the first unclouded beam of the uncreated light, as though lightning-struck; for no mortal being, however eagle-eyed, may behold a God and live, as the Greeks said of old. Thus when Moses asked for the same revelation, there came to him the answer, "I will *make My goodness pass before thee.*" Elijah's hearing, deeper down than in the storm and the earthquake, the still small voice of conscience, is but a type of man's advance in evolution from being the mere passive recipient of God's goodness to having become aware that only the pure in heart can see God, only the loving can love Him, and only the wise can obey Him. Were it but taught and learnt that our happiness lies in the power of mutual love, in the intelligising the order of the universe which we inhabit, and in the consecration of our will to harmony with the Divine will, instead of in the vain endeavour to ignore our own Being, and disregard our own wellbeing, the " formal apparatus of thought " being thus respected, we should be nearer to truth, harmony, and goodness than any self-illusion, or delusion of others, through persuading them that we prefer their happiness to our own, can possibly bring us. Surely also a God devoid of self-consciousness or personality such as we have in Pantheism would put the human instinct of prayer logically out of court, seeing that faith, love, and hope apply only to the attributes of Being or personality, but for us possibly to arrive at complete faithlessness, loveless- ness, and hopelessness—we must first have achieved the paralysis of all our faculties, and then there would indeed exist a rational ground or standpoint for Agnosticism and despair.

> " Night lies upon the deep, the vasty deep,
>   With headlands, shoals, and rocks to fear,
> Yet sailors cast no anchor, take no sleep,
>   But still *by chart and compass steer.*
>
> Sight is a fitful moonbeam on our sea
>   To charm us, not to teach us what to do.
> He who would gain the port must ever be,
>   In light and dark, *to chart and compass true.*"

THE END.

PRINTED BY BALLANTYNE, HANSON AND CO.
EDINBURGH AND LONDON.

www.ingramcontent.com/pod-product-compliance
Lightning Source LLC
Chambersburg PA
CBHW020014030726
47500CB00002B/576